THE MADONNAS OF EUROPE

*The publishers would like
to thank the following
companies whose
assistance made
this book possible:*

The Ministry
of Culture and Art
of the Republic of Poland

Kodak Poland

The Pallotine
Travel Bureau

British Airways

The National Tourism
Organisation of Malta

THE MADONNAS OF EUROPE

Janusz Rosikoń

Rosikon press

CONTENTS

FOREWORD

As we enter the third Millennium, humanity seeks new horizons, new ideas, sometimes making the world around us a friendlier place and allowing us to rediscover those forgotten values which enrich our existence, so it becomes more meaningful and better.

In honouring the 2000th anniversary of the birth of Christ, the Church recognises in the Blessed Virgin Mary a perfect example of a Christian way of life, filled with deep faith and true love for all people.

May this book celebrating the shrines where the Virgin is venerated throughout Europe, from the Atlantic Ocean to the Urals, bear testimony to our beliefs and devotion to the Mother of God, who will guide us and support us with Her power and might on the path into the next Millennium, enabling us to meet and overcome the challenges of the times in which, through God's will, we live on this Earth.

+ Cardinal Józef Glemp
Primate of Poland

Warsaw
The Feast of the Annunciation
Anno Domini 1998

MARIAN SANCTUARIES

When I retired after many years of work as Head of the Papal Council on Communications, the Holy Father placed me at the helm of the International Pontifical Marian Academy, which studies the dogmas concerning the Mother of God and Her veneration by the faithful. The Academy consists of scholars who specialise in Mariology and lay people, mainly young, who are involved in the ministry of the Church. The great task of spreading the Gospel in the modern world through the influence of Marian sanctuaries has become an essential part of my assignment. Europe has been 'the land of the Mother of God' for many centuries, so shrines devoted to Her can be found all over the continent, from the Urals to Portugal and from Ireland to Malta. The impetus for their creation came from the spriual need of both the Eastern and Western Church. They offer proof of the deep faith of all European nations, and for hundreds of years they have played the role of bastions defending Christianity in Europe.

Even in our own times Europe has been the location of several appearances by the Virgin Mary. She comes to places where She is loved and needed, and these visitations confirm Europe's desire for Her love and protection.

Despite some pessimistic predictions, Marian veneration shows no signs of weakening. On the contrary, Her sanctuaries have turned into islands emanating spirituality and continue to attract enormous groups of believers. I am in constant touch with their curators who inform me that the number of pilgrims is increasing steadily and that many of them are young. Particularly with the latter in mind, the International Pontifical Marian Academy has set up the

so-called Houses of the Virgin Mary, attached to the sanctuaries, where visitors can obtain information on the shrines themselves, as well as places to stay, the time of religious services, confessions and Masses in different languages. Their main role is to provide spiritual guidance, which helps the pilgrims to derive greater benefit from their journey and encounter with the Mother of God. Such centres already exist in Lourdes, Fatima, Loreto and Częstochowa.

Here I would like to quote the words of Pope John Paul II about the importance of Marian sanctuaries, spoken when he was still Archbishop of Cracow: 'Sanctuaries are the Church's capital, because they are the focal points from which the Word of God is proclaimed and where the sacraments are celebrated, where prayers are held and the Church congregates on a stage greater than a parish. They are the site where pilgrim's experiences merge with the life of the Virgin, and the experiences of the nation, the country and every region with the unceasing love of the Church and its Mother.'

I warmly welcome the initiative of the Ave Maria Foundation which led to the publication of this book on Marian sanctuaries in Europe. The photographs of Janusz Rosikoń show both the sanctuaries which are known to all and many less familiar ones, scattered throughout our continent. One has to rejoice in the fact that *The Madonnas of Europe* will enable readers to undertake a spiritual pilgrimage to the shrines where different European nations venerate the Virgin Mary.

† Cardinal Andrzej Maria Deskur

PREFACE

Two photographs by Janusz Rosikoń can be found in my family home. One of them shows a tranquil monastic scene. The other, a dynamic portrait of Pope John Paul II holding aloft the crucifix, hangs in the place of honour above the bed of our younger son, Christian. We bought those pictures several years ago after seeing them in a public exhibition. I am an unabashed admirer of Rosikoń's work.

When I was a child, I was tought that religious images had no part in a serious spiritual life. My mother, who was a highly devout and principled lady and an active member of her Protestant Church, warned me in particular against the cult of the Virgin Mary. In her eyes, as in the eyes of most Protestants, the Marian cult had no basis in Holy Scripture and was seen as a dubious invention of the institutionalised Church. As such, it is thought to divert the attention of Christian believers from the one and only true object of their Faith, namely Jesus Christ Himself. One was encouraged to adore the Holy Family, particularly at Christmas time, but not to pay special attention to the Blessed Virgin. Music held a prominent place in Protestant worship, not least through those magnificent Welsh hymns. But icons and visual images did not. As a young historian, I knew that the fury of Protestant rulers in sixteenth and seventeenth century England, especially of the regicide Lord Protector, Oliver Cromwell, had caused the physical destruction of almost all the country's Marian shrines and other saintly images. Most of them have never been replaced. Of course, I frequently saw paintings of the Mother and Child. I was fortunate to be taken to Florence and Rome as a schoolboy and to see some of the glorious Madonnas of Raphael, Titian and Michaelangelo. But we were invited to admire them intellectually as great art, not as an internal spiritual experience.

With time, both my mind and my heart changed. My youthful travels round Europe gave me a new perspective on our continent's religious traditions. I saw Notre Dame and Chartres and Lourdes and Montserrat, and eventually both Potchaiev and Kiev. I once found myself camping in a parish garden at an alpine village in Austria, which for Britishers had been 'enemy territory' only ten years before. And nothing set me thinking more deeply than the wonderful music, Catholic devotion and friendly conversation of

the priest in the simplest of rural churches. I was twenty-three years old before I visited Poland, and at Jasna Góra felt the immense magnetic power which the *Matka Boska* exercised over everyone present. I attended a pilgrimage to Kalwaria Lanckorońska, and saw the social bonding which such occasions create. With much greater delay, I knelt before the *Matka Boska Ostrobramska*. So, I eventually found myself 'in Rome', in all senses of the phrase. Now, as a member of the Roman Catholic community, I can finally value the Virgin Mother of God as an essential and effective figure both in the Christian Faith and in the long history of Europe. It was in such a spirit that I devoted a number of pages on 'The Madonna' in my recent book *Europe: a History* to the four 'Black Madonnas' of Montserrat, Częstochowa, Rocamadour, and Kazań.

It is hard for Poles to fully appreciate the wider role of the Marian Cult. They live in a country where the Blessed Virgin was venerated from an early date and where, indeed, She was raised to the status of 'Queen of Heaven, Queen of Poland'. She is part of their national cosmos. Only when they go abroad, can they see how much they share with Europe's other peoples. This Album, *The Madonnas of Europe* by Janusz Rosikoń and Wojciech Niżyński will help to achieve that realisation.

The Madonnas of Europe, and the inspiration behind Them, underline three important facts. Firstly, They show that Christianity is a universal Faith, not a national one. Secondly, They show that the Eastern Orthodox Church is a vital and prominent partner in that universal company. Thirdly, They emphasise that the ecumenical solidarityof all Christian believers offers the surest path of Hope in continent whose technological achievements have far outstripped its spiritual consciousness.

Norman Davies F.B.A., P.A.U.

Oxford, March 1998

[1] *Europe a History*, Oxford University Press, 1996.

First published Warsaw 1998
English edition published Warsaw 2000

Rosikon press
Grażyna Kasprzycka-Rosikoń

Consultants:
Rev Dr Kazimierz Kurek SDB
Rev Dr Mieczysław Maliński
Rev Fr Jan Pach PhD OSPPE
Rev Dr Henryk Paprocki
Rev Dr Jan Pawlik
Rev Prof Krzysztof Pawlina
Rev Dr Teofil Siudy

Editors
Marianna Domańska
Teresa Sobańska-Dąbrowska
Andrzej Ziemilski

English translation and editing
Natalia von Svolkien

Consultant for English edition
Father William M. McLoughlin OSM

Proof-reading
Brian Eggar

Research
Teresa Czerkawska

DTP Consult
Maryla Broda

Cartography
Ewa Jurek

© Photography
Janusz Rosikoń

© Rosikon press 1998
al. Dębów 4, 05-080 Izabelin-Warsaw
e-mail rosikon@ikp.atm.com.pl
tel. (+48 22) 722 6101, fax (+48 22) 722 6667

ISBN 83-903459-2-7 (Polish edition)
ISBN 83-903459-7-8 (English edition)

Production consultant
Leo Chu Chun Wan

Printed by
Sun Funfg Offset China

Kielce: *'Totus tuus'* – this
definition of a bishop's
calling, formulated by
Karol Wojtyła, now
Pope John Paul II, is proof
of his veneration of the Virgin
Mary. The photograph shows
the Pope during his pilgrimage
to the country where he was
born. On 3 June 1991
he crowned the miraculous
image of the Virgin Mary
of Mercy. The painting
can be found in the
cathedral in Kielce.

PORTUGAL
SPAIN
FRANCE

PORTUGAL
SPAIN
FRANCE

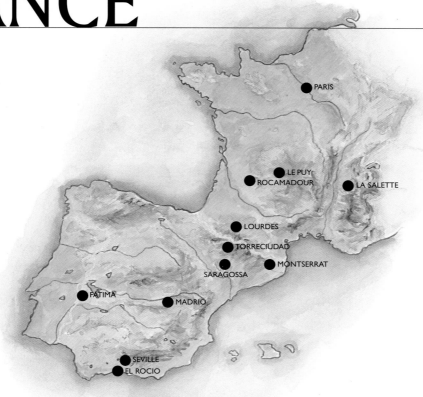

It is a well-known truth that the hot climate of the Mediterranean strongly affects the character and temperament of the people who live there. Their blood seems to flow quicker, and they tend to wear their hearts on their sleeves. Those who love, love madly, with no holds barred; those who play do so without much care for their bank balance or of tomorrow; those who pray, pray fervently. This is a land of extremes. Its inhabitants often let their hearts rule their heads, and momentary feelings frequently count for more than cool reasoning.

Seville (left):
Nuestra Señora de los Reyes, which means Our of the Kings Lady, is the Patron Saint of Seville and all of Andalucia. The small sculpture was made of larch wood either in the thirteenth century, or at the turn of the fourteenth. It can be found in the Chapel Royal of the Seville Cathedral. Whenever the ruling monarch or members of the Spanish royal family visit Seville, in accordance with an old custom, they pray in this chapel for their own well-being and for the country.

Saragossa (preceding pages):
On the Feast Day of the Flowers, the people of Aragón, accompanied by music and singing, come to see their Patron Saint. To the sound of castanets, they dance the traditional *jotas,* the local folk dances, which are an intrinsic expression of their temperament. Later, on the stage situated at the foot of the basilica and surrounded by a sea of flowers, they sing songs glorifying Our Lady of Pilar. These songs are full of joy and unrestrained expression.

When one stands in front of the monastery at Belém in Lisbon, next to the sailors' monument and facing the estuary of the Tagus river as it flows into the Atlantic, there is no doubt that this is the true gateway of Europe. The curiosity about the unknown which awaited them beyond the far blue horizon, made the great explorers set off on their voyages. The first men who discovered new lands for the Europeans were all Portugese: Henry 'the Navigator', Bartolomeo Dias, Vasco da Gama and Ferdinand Magellan. Prior to leaving on their dangerous journeys, they would kneel before the statue of the Mother of God at Belém and promise that they would advance the veneration for the Virgin all over the world. The missionaries, who were following in their footsteps, spread the word of God to overseas territories. *Stella Maris,* the Star of the Sea, as the Virgin was referred to, the Patron Saint of sailors and fishermen, watched over and guarded their tasks.

The strong tradition of the veneration for the Mother of God which like a golden thread winds itself through the entire history of Portugal, gives the country every right to call itself 'the realm of the Virgin Mary'. The love bestowed on Her by the Portugese is full of the burning passion of the South, and at the same time extremely open and tender. The first Portugese king, Don Afonso I, put the country in Her care, naming Her the Protectress and Mother of Portugal. Before Don Afonso met the Moors in battle at Santar, he vowed that if he were granted victory, he would build a monastery where monks would for ever sing in praise of the Virgin. He kept his promise and in 1152 began the construction of a magnificent monastery at Alcobaça for the Cisterians that he had brought over from France. According to tradition, since Don Afonso's times all Portuguese rulers took with them to the field of battle the statue of the Mother of God.

Portugal had to fight for its independence on more than one occasion, first with the Moors, and later with the kingdom of León and Castile. To commemorate the battle at Aljubarrota in 1385, King Don João I founded in Batalha a Dominican monastery, one of the true masterpieces of Gothic art. The monasteries at Alcobaça and Batalha, which have been centres of Marian worship for hundreds of years, are close to Fatima. In 1917, this little, unknown village became the location of the most important pronouncement made by the Mother of God in the twentieth century. She spoke to three Portugese children, but Her message was addressed to all humanity and to every generation. She urged people to repent of their sins and to reform their lives. Portugal paid heed to these words and between 1931 and 1940 on three separate occasions the country was dedicated to the Immaculate Heart of the Virgin. The Portugese are seeking guidance with a rosary in their hands, just as the Mother of God has asked them to do.

Małgorzata Rutkowska

Fatima: The pavement along which the faithful approach the Chapel of Revelations is six hundred and sixty feet long. In April 1919 a small chapel was built from stone near the oak in which the Virgin Mary appeared to three children: ten year old Lucia dos Santos, nine year old Francisco Marto and his cousin, Jacinta Marto, who was seven years old. The votive statue of the Virgin, based on the children's description of Her, was made in cedar wood by José Ferreira Thedima and placed in the chapel. It was funded by the man who was restored to health at the time of the revelations.

Fatima: The Mother of God appeared to the children for the first time on 13 May 1917. Later, they said 'She was dressed in white, and brighter than the sun. The light was purer and more intense than the rays of the sun shining through a crystal goblet of water.' 'The lady in white' asked Lucia, Jacinta and Franco to return five more times, on the thirteenth day of each month. She also instructed them to say the rosary every day, in order to pray for an end of the First World War.

Fatima: Neither the rain nor the sun stop the faithful from coming here. When the Virgin appeared to the children for the third time, on 13 July 1917, She revealed to them the so-called 'Mystery of Fatima'. It consisted of three parts. The first concerned the fate of the three children, and the second presented a vision of hell and the way to salvation through prayer to the Immaculate Heart of the Virgin. The third part is only known to successive Popes.

Fatima: The statue of Our Lady of Fatima travels all over the world. Here it can be seen before its journey to Poland in October 1995, followed by men from the mountain region in the south of the country, wearing their traditional folk costumes. The pilgrimages of the Travelling Madonna were inaugurated on 13 May 1940, on the thirtieth anniversary of the revelations. Four copies of the statue of the Pilgrim Madonna were made in Fatima, following the instructions of Sister Lucia, and specially blessed by priests. They traversed Europe on their way to Africa, Asia, Oceania and both Americas. The first pilgrimage began with a visit to Maastricht in Holland.
The voyages of 1978 and 1983 took the statue to many places throughout the world.

Fatima: Nearly seventy thousand
pilgrims from across Portugal came
to Fatima on 13 October 1917,
to watch the sixth appearance of the
Virgin there. They witnessed an
extraordinary phenomenon, which
lasted for ten minutes. The sun began
to vibrate rapidly round its axis,
and then it moved across the sky
following a zig-zag route,
as if it were dancing. Finally, emitting
multi-coloured rays, like a burning
sphere it started to roll down over
the crowd.

Fatima: One of the many religious centres connected with the
veneration of Our Lady of Fatima is *Domus Pacis* (the House of Peace),
the European headquarters of the Blue Army, also known
as the World Apostolate of Fatima. Officially recognised by Pope Pius
XII in 1947, the Blue Army was founded by the Rev Harold Colgan,
a parish priest in New Jersey, USA. Nowadays it has millions
of members all over the world.

Fatima: Many of the pilgrims are ill or disabled. They are looked after by specially set-up medical services. During his visit to Fatima in May 1991, Pope John Paul II prayed 'Mother of hope, as we approach the end of the twentieth century, keep us company on our way, whatever our race, cultural background, social class and age may be.'

Fatima: From the facade of the basilica, the Virgin Mary welcomes all pilgrims, reminding them to say the rosary every day. The statue was made by an American monk, named Thomas McGlynn. In Fatima the Mother of God predicted the collapse of the Communist rule in Europe and the revival of religious faith in Russia. She said that it would happen after the world, and Russia in particular, had become dedicated to Her Immaculate Heart. On 25 March 1984 a special Act of Faith was proclaimed in Rome by Pope John Paul II, in the presence of the miraculous statue from Fatima.

Fatima: Since the second appearance of the Virgin Mary, the Cova da Iria valley has been visited by countless pilgrims. Nowadays about six million of them arrive here every year from all over the world. As early as 1930 the Catholic Church recognised the revelations as being worthy of belief. A year later, the first national pilgrimage to Fatima was organised. It was joined by a million participants. During the celebrations the bishops placed Portugal in the special care of the Virgin's Immaculate Heart.

Fatima: The basilica was consecrated in October 1953. It contains the tombs of the children who witnessed the revelations: Jacinta, who died in 1919 and Franco, whose death occurred in 1920. The beatification process of the two little shepherds is currently taking place. The nearby Byzantine chapel Domus Pacis houses the priceless icon of Our Lady of Kazan, which for centuries has been venerated in Rus'. It is seen as a symbol of the Christian roots of the Russian nation. A copy of the Black Madonna from Częstochowa in Poland can also be seen there.

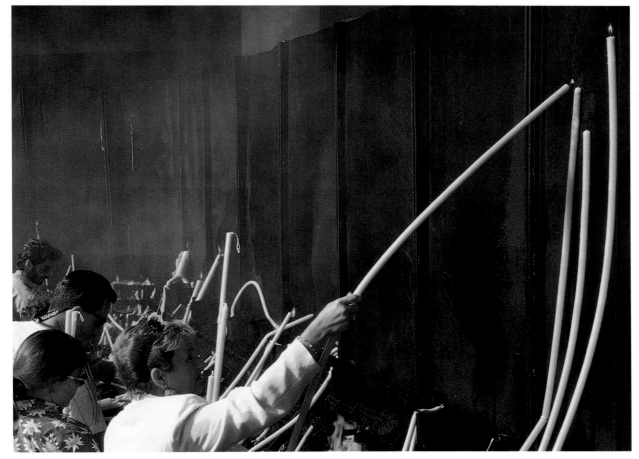

Fatima: The votive candles are burning at the site of the revelations. Of the three children who witnessed them, only Lucia is still alive. She is a nun at the Carmelite convent in Coimbra.

Fatima: For years, the pilgrims have been moving along the path of repentance on their knees. They follow in the footsteps of Lucia, who prayed here to the Virgin, imploring Her to restore the health of her mother. The girl promised Madonna that for nine consecutive days she would work her way on her knees to the oak where the revelations occurred. After three days, Lucia's mother began to feel better and soon she had completely recovered. When the Virgin appeared to Lucia twelve years later, on 13 June 1929, She reminded the young woman of Her wish, expressed in Fatima: 'The moment has come when God demands that the Holy Father and all the bishops of the world should dedicate Russia to my Immaculate Heart.'

Fatima: The terrazzo paving stones, polished by the knees of the pilgrims, shine like true marble from Carrara. The path leads to the site of the revelations. Since the autumn days of 1989, when the Communist regimes of Central and Eastern Europe collapsed, the number of visitors from that part of the world has been increasing steadily. In July 1995 the head of the Catholic Church in Belarus, Kazimierz Świątek, proclaimed here an Act of Faith in Our Lady of Fatima. He spent many years as a prisoner in Soviet labour camps. In October 1996 the Catholic bishops of Russia paid homage to the Virgin Mary.

Fatima: In October 1996, the faithful are saying good-bye to the statue, before it is sent on another pilgrimage, through 'the Gulag Archipelago', where hundreds of thousands perished in Soviet concentration camps, then Katyn – the site of the barbaric murder of Polish army officers by the NKVD in 1940, later Ekaterinburg, where the last Tsar, Nicholas II and his family were killed in July 1918 on Lenin's orders, and finally great battlefields and places of massacres from the Second World War.

Fatima: Among the precious stones set in the crown of Our Lady of Fatima there is a spent bullet offered in gratitude by Pope John Paul II on the tenth anniversary of the attempt on his life, which took place on 13 May 1981. This bullet which managed to wound but not kill him, is seen by many to be more valuable than all the jewels in this crown.

Warsaw: In October 1995, the statue of the Virgin Mary from Fatima arrived at Warsaw airport. The men from the mountain region in the south, together with their mayor from Zakopane, Adam Bachleda-Caruś and Father Mirosław Drozdek took part in greeting the Virgin on Polish land. The journey through Poland lasted a year, and took in all the Catholic dioceses.

Zakopane: In the sanctuary of Our Lady of Fatima on Krzeptówki, at the base of Giewont, one of the most famous peaks in the Tatra Mountains, the local people and the Pallotine Fathers welcomed the Pilgrim Madonna in December 1995. In 1961 the statue of Our Lady of Fatima was given by the Bishop of Fatima to the Polish Primate Stefan Wyszyński, who in turn offered it to the chapel of the Pallotines in Zakopane. It was the first copy of the statue from Fatima which entered Poland officially. The sanctuary on Krzeptówki was built to thank the Virgin Mary for the miraculous deliverance of the Holy Father from an attempted assassination in 1981. Continuous prayers for the Pope are held in this beautiful church, a masterpiece of the region's folk art. John Paul II consecrated it during special celebrations on 7 June 1997, the year of his fifth pilgrimage to Poland.

Moscow: Only a short while ago, could anyone have imagined that the statue of Our Lady of Fatima would journey across Russia, and that one day people would pay homage to it in the Red Square, near the mausoleum of Lenin, father of the Bolshevik revolution who made the fight against religion one of the main tenets of his ideology?

Perm: 'If my wishes are fulfilled, Russia will return to its faith and peace will follow', said the Virgin Mary when She appeared at Fatima for the third time. Many years later, it became obvious that Her words were prophetic: the churches all over Russia once again filled with believers. Here both Catholic and Orthodox priests carry the statue of Our Lady of Fatima, which during its great pilgrimage through Russia arrived also at Perm in the Urals, only a few miles from the eastern border of Europe.

The irregular, pentagonal shape of the Iberian Peninsula is compared by its inhabitants to the hide of a bull, *una piel de toro.* Like Portugal, Spain was often called 'the land of the Virgin Mary', and this description of it still reflects the truth about the people who live there, their characters and mentality. The Spaniards, Catalonians and Basques, despite all the differences between them, echoing the geographical variety of the land (the hot, sunny south and the misty, cloudy north), find themselves united in their love of the *Virgen* – the Virgin, as they call the Mother of God, imitating in this Saint Ildefonsus of Toledo.

There is no area of Spain where at least one Marian sanctuary cannot be found, in fact there are many towns where every area has chosen Her for its Patron Saint. The Catalonians go on pilgrimages to Montserrat, reigned over by *la Moreneta;* the Andalusians travel to Seville, to *la Macarena;* the Asturians, whose region gave birth to Spanish statehood, set off for Covadonga, where in 718 the Moors were defeated in battle by Christian knights. The victory was attributed to the intercession of the Virgin Mary. Right from the beginning of Christianity, the cave in the Covadonga Mountains (derived from *Cova Dominae* – the Lady's Cave in Latin) was dedicated to the Mother of God.

History decreed that through its great explorers Spain was able to carry the Christian faith to the New World, beginning in 1492, the year of Columbus's arrival in America. The Patron Saint of the vast Spanish-speaking territories on that continent is Our Lady of Pilar from Saragossa Cathedral – *Virgen del Pilar.*

According to tradition, the basilica in Saragossa stands at the site of the oldest Marian sanctuary in Spain: it is said that in the year 40, the Virgin Mary arrived in Caesaragusta, as the capital of Aragón used to be called in Roman times, in order to meet, console and encourage the Apostle Saint James the Great in his missionary work. She was supposed to have pointed out the location where a chapel should be built in Her honour.

Although Spain is often referred to as 'the land of Saint James the Great', whose supposed tomb at

Seville: Such scenes can be observed in Seville quite often during *Semana Santa* (Holy Week). A quiet, deserted street at daybreak and a lonely *nazareno,* a member of one of the brotherhoods, resembling a strange prehistoric bird with a long beak. He is probably on the way to join a procession at his parish.

Santiago de Compostela is an important source of national identity, love and veneration for the Virgin Mary are still a particularly Spanish trait. The youth of Spain, fond of singing, quick and lively in its reactions, can usually be found at the forefront of any great religious celebrations. It has always remained faithful to the Church.

Some people maintain that the antiphon *Salve Regina,* the most popular prayer to the Virgin after *Ave Maria*, could have been written nowhere else but in Spain, by Saint Peter of Mezomo, the Bishop of Compostela at the end of the tenth century. Today ninety seven per cent of Spain's population is Catholic – it must be partly due to its Marian traditions and inheritance, which have influenced the Iberian civilization so profoundly.

Wojciech Niżyński

Seville: *La Macarena,* the Virgin Mary of Hope, is the most loved Madonna statue among those which are venerated in the processions of Holy Week. The magnificent sculpture with diamond tears on the cheeks derives its name from the poor, working-class district of western Seville, where it is housed in a basilica. The *Macarena* Madonna is also the Patron Saint of matadors, as the word *macareno* describes someone who is bold and brave.

Seville: Almost every statue of the Virgin carried in the processions is dressed in magnificent robes, embroided with golden thread and embellished with precious stones. The tears visible on the face are an expression of pain and despair after the death of Her Son. The canopy held above the Madonna is made of an equally valuable cloth and supported by intricate columns cast in silver.

Seville: Every area of the town has its own Madonna. Dressed in sumptous garments and crowned with a glorious crown, She is greeted everywhere by thousands of believers, who see Her as their Mother and Patron Saint.

Seville: The robes may be black, purple, green, red or white – their secret, symbolic language is only fully understood by the inhabitants of Seville. The colours tell them which *paso* (portable altar) is going to appear next. Crowds of the faithful and a large number of tourists come to Seville to admire this miracle play, a mixture of religion and street theatre. For outsiders it always retains an element of mystery, leaving some questions unanswered.

Seville: *Semana Santa,* (Holy Week), apart from providing a magnificent display of altars crowned with the statues of the Virgin Mary, concentrates on the story of Christ and serves as a reminder of His suffering and death on the cross. Altars with scenes of the Crucifixion are carried in some of the street processions. They are accompanied by members of penitentiary societies, who carry enormous black crosses on their shoulders.

Seville: The famous Campana is the square through which all the processions carrying *paso* have to pass. Stands covered with red cloth are placed on both sides of the square. Members of the patrician families of Seville have been occupying the same seats for generations.

Seville: On Maundy Thursday, in this narrowest of streets, San Vicente, whole families gather even on really tiny balconies, like birds on a perch. They want to watch *paso* leaving the Church of Saint Anthony.

Seville: The tradition of joining societies which are active in the parishes is passed from father to son. During the processions of Holy Week boys of just a few years can be seen walking by the side of their fathers, wearing traditional costumes and filled with awe by the importance of the occasion.

Seville: The altar stops after every few hundred yards. The *costaleros* who carry it, are replaced by new ones. Their heads are wrapped to minimise the risk of injury. When the bell or the metal rattle sounds, the altar is raised and the procession starts again. The drums dictate the speed of the march and changes of direction.

Seville: On the stroke of midnight on Good Friday, one of the most spectacular processions of Seville's *Semana Santa* leaves the Basilica del Gran Poder. The appearance of the *paso* in the doorway is preceded by a long lane of *nazarenos* in their white robes. The light of the candles and the torches they carry disperses the darkness in the wooded square before the basilica.

Seville: Holy Saturday is spent with the family. It is a day free from work. People in their best clothes visit the churches, then meet in the bars and cafés. Women look particularly elegant on that day: they wear *peinetas,* special, high combs on top of their heads. These combs are often made of tortoiseshell and are very valuable. Black lace veils which flow down from the combs onto the women's shoulders are worn as a sign of mourning for the death of Christ.

El Rocio: The sixteenth century sanctuary is an object of ardent love by the local people, who venerate and adore the statue of *Nuestra Señora del Rocio,* which means 'covered with dew'. On Whit Sunday it is visited by thousands of people who live in the Andalusian countryside.

Seville (preceding page):
In the capital of Andalusia, the statue of the Virgin Mary at the cathedral stands on the biggest wooden altar in the world. It is sixty six foot high, a true masterpiece of the wood carver's art. It is the fruit of labour of over twenty outstanding artists from different European countries, who between 1482 and 1564 created thousands of figures which are grouped together into fortyfive scenes from the life of the Holy Family. There are also statues of the Patron Saints of the town. On the days of *Corpus Christi* and the Immaculate Conception of the Virgin Mary, the Liturgy celebrated at this altar is accompanied by traditional Andalusian songs and dances, including the bolero, sung by a boys choir dressed in sixteenth century costumes.

El Rocio: Among the pilgrims there are also horse riders, who come to pay homage to the Madonna. Every seven years the statue is dressed in a sombrero and the folk costume of the local shepherds. It is carried in a procession, organised by the Marian Brotherhood from El Rocio. The King of Spain is an honorary member.

El Rocio: According to an old legend, in the sixteenth century the Gothic statue of *Nuestra Señora del Rocio,* Our Lady of Dew, was found by a hunter in nearby woods. Local people call Her *Paloma Bianca* (the White Dove), because the main feast at the sanctuary falls on the day of the Descent of the Holy Spirit.

Madrid: La Almudena Cathedral. Its construction, begun in 1868, took over a hundred years. The cathedral was consecrated by Pope John Paul II on 15 June 1993.

Madrid: La Almudena Cathedral. The eighteen panels of the altar were painted in the sixteenth century by Juan de Borgoña, court painter of Emperor Carlos V. They were placed in the funerary chapel of the Archangel Michael in Toledo. Following the creation of the new of archdiocese Madrid-Alcalá, the altar was moved to the seat of the diocese in Madrid.

Madrid: La Almudena Cathedral. The statue of the Mother of God was made at the turn of the fifteenth century by an unknown sculptor. The veneration of the *la Almudena* Virgin dates back to much earlier times. The first document in which She is mentioned comes from 1377. On 10 November 1948 in Plaza de la Armeria the statue was ceremoniously crowned and the *la Almudena* Madonna was proclaimed the Patron Saint of Madrid.

Saragossa: At night, on the eve of the Feast Day
of Our Lady of Pilar, in the square in front of the basilica,
a big *fiesta* takes place, with folk ensembles and singers.
It ends with thousands of fireworks exploding over the
towers and cupolas of the basilica and scattering down like
a cascade of colourful, flickering stars.

Saragossa: The miraculous
statue of Our Lady of Pilar
measures only fifteen inches.
It is placed on top of a pillar
which reaches almost six feet six
inches in height. The pillar is a relic
from the ancient sanctuary which
was considered to be one of the
first churches in the world
dedicated to the veneration
of the Virgin Mary. It was built
in the place where the Mother
of God appeared before the
Apostle James the Great.
Nowadays the pillar is barely
visible underneath the votive
garments, which are changed
every day throughout the year.

Saragossa: Countless multitudes pour down Afonso I Street in the direction of the basilica on the river Ebro, to see the miniature statue of the Mother of God, which has been adored by the inhabitants of Aragón since the earliest days of Christianity. When the procession comes to an end, all that is left is a carpet of flowers, hundreds of feet long.

Saragossa: A boy in a wheelchair is one of a crowd of half a million who have come to pay homage to the Patron Saint of Aragón. Our Lady of Pilar is famous for the so-called miracle of Calanda. Twenty year old Miguel Juan Pellicer used to pray fervently and rub the oil which came from the lamps placed before the statue of the Virgin Mary into the stump of his amputated leg. On the night of 29 March 1640 the leg grew back miraculously.

Saragossa: On October 12, the Feast Day of Our Lady of Pilar, the people of Saragossa and the whole region of Aragón place armfuls of flowers at the feet of a copy of the miraculous statue, brought outside the basilica. 'Masters of ceremony' arrange the flowers on racks, creating a magnificent cloak of white carnations and gladioli.

Montserrat: The name means 'the saw mountain' in Spanish and is derived from the serrated outline of the peak, which rises abruptly from a Catalonian plain to 4,054 feet. The eighth century sanctuary is one of the oldest dedicated to the Virgin Mary in this part of Europe. At present, there is a church and a celebrated Benedictine monastery more than half way up the precipitous cliffs. In the Middle Ages, pilgrims used to stop here on their way to Santiago de Compostela.

Montserrat: For centuries, pilgrims have travelled to Montserrat from the whole of Spain and from many countries of Europe. Among the first names listed in the monastery chronicles is Ignatius Loyola, the future founder of the Jesuit Order. Here, at Montserrat, following a period of prayer, he exchanged the splendid armour of a knight for monk's robes.

Montserrat: Every day, the worshippers stop before Our Lady of Montserrat and kiss or touch the wooden orb in the Virgin's hand, the symbol of royal power. It is the only part of the statue not concealed by glass. According to legend, the statue was carved by Saint Luke, and Saint Peter was supposed to have brought it to Spain.

Montserrat: *La Moreneta* – the Little Black Girl – is the tender name given to their statue of the Virgin Mary by the people of Montserrat, on account of the colour of the faces of Mary and the Infant Christ, the natural shade of old wood. The rest of the Byzantine-Romanesque statue is covered with goldleaf. Every day, at one o'clock in the afternoon, students from the local conservatoire sing the anthipon *Salve Regina* here.

Torreciudad: This sanctuary in the Spanish Pyrenees was opened on July 7, 1975. It was created on the initiative of Opus Dei, who continue to look after it. However, the veneration of the Virgin Mary in this place, situated half way between El Pilar in Saragossa and Lourdes, dates back to the eleventh century. At the time, having conquered a fortress which belonged to the Muslims, the Christians placed a statue of the Mother of God in the local chapel.

Torreciudad: This magnificent high altar in Torreciudad was sculpted in alabaster by Juan Mayné. It contains eight panels with scenes from the Virgin's life. Its form was influenced by the Renaissance style of the Aragón region.

Torreciudad: This Romanesque wooden sculpture from the eleventh century represents the Mother of God as the Queen of Angels. Thanks to Her intercession, Josemaria Escrivá de Balaguer was miraculously restored to health in 1904. He later founded Opus Dei and was beatified in 1992.

France is justly proud of its title 'the eldest daughter of the Church'. Since the days of Clovis, who together with his retinue accepted baptism from the hands of Saint Remi, at some point between 496 and 506, thus making Gaul the first country after the demise of the Roman Empire to join the European Christian community, throughout the centuries its Church has played a crucial role in influencing the nature of universal Catholicism. The process took place on several levels: from close connections with the Holy See (as many as seventeen Popes have come from the territories which today constitute France), through the enormous significance of French philosophical and theological thought and a host of great saints, to the cultural impact of Paris.

French piety has always been strongly marked by its veneration for the Virgin Mary, particularly in the twelfth century, which became known as 'the age of cathedrals', because of many cathedrals built and dedicated to the Mother of God. It was also the time when the tradition of pilgrimages to Marian sanctuaries grew in strength. As early as the sixth century, worshippers began visiting Chartres, where they not only prayed beside the highly venerated statue of the Virgin, but also admired 'the stole of the Mother of God', offered by the Carolingian King, Charles the Bald. In 1935 French students initiated their increasingly popular annual pilgrimages from the Notre-Dame Cathedral in Paris to Chartres.

Before Lourdes, le Puy was the most famous Marian sanctuary in France. In 1095 Pope Urban II set off from there to Clermont, to announce the first Crusade, when he was supposed to have said 'The Kingdom of France is the kingdom of the Virgin Mary: it will never perish!' In the thirteenth century the act of dedicating his realm to the Mother of God was performed by Saint Louis, and repeated by Louis XIII four hundred years later. The veneration of the Mother of God found an even deeper expression in *True Devotion to the Blessed Virgin,* a book written by Saint Louis Maria Grignion de Montfort.

The development of the French Church was severely checked by the Revolution of 1789. It brought with

La Salette: The Basilica of the Blessed Virgin Mary nestles between the bare Alpine peaks at nearly six thousand feet above sea level, like a place of refuge to lost wanderers. The Virgin has been venerated here since Her appearance on 19 September 1846.

it persecution of the clergy and destruction of many churches and monasteries. It also led to the permanent separation of the Church and State in French political life. In the circumstances, it may be difficult to fathom why in the nineteenth century France was chosen as a place for repeated appearances of the Virgin Mary and Her great proclamations, beginning with Paris in 1830, then la Salette in 1846, and finally Lourdes in 1858. The sanctuaries which grew up around the locations visited by the Virgin are now living centres of faith, where many people renew their belief in God, and the French Catholic Church redefines its identity, weakened by the crises of the last few decades. Consequently, and not for the first time, the Catholic world finds itself greatly indebted to France, the eldest daughter of the Church.

Małgorzata Rutkowska

La Salette: The statue shows the Virgin Mary as the Help of Sinners. She chose two poor shepherds, fifteen years old Melanie Calvat and eleven year old Maxim Giraud, to pass on Her message, calling for people's spiritual rebirth. The Beautiful Lady is clad in the traditional attire of peasant women from Savoy, a white dress with a yellow apron and a shawl on Her shoulders. From Her neck hang a golden cross and implements of the Passion. With the face sunk into Her hands, she resembles a caring mother, pondering the fate of Her children.

La Salette: On the Feast Day of the Patron Saint of the sanctuary, 19 September, a Mass is said in front of the basilica. The basilica was consecrated in 1879. In the same year, Our Lady of la Salette was crowned. The Crying Madonna was deeply venerated by Saint Jean-Marie Vianney and Saint John Bosco.

La Salette: Over 200,000 pilgrims come here every year to pray at the sanctuary. The first anniversary of the Virgin Mary's appearance drew at least thirty thousand believers to the Holy Mountain, at whose foot springs a miraculous source of water. A foundation stone for the basilica was laid in 1852.

La Salette: The statue shows Melanie Calvat and Maxim Giraud talking to the Virgin Mary. 'Come closer, children, do not be afraid. I am here to tell you important news', said the Virgin in the shepherds' vision, all the time crying over 'poor sinners' and the misfortunes which befall them and cause their anger, rather than being seen as an urgent call to return to God.

Paris: The embalmed body of Saint Catherine Labouré rests in the chapel of the Sisters of Charity at 140 rue du Bac. In 1830 she had several visions of the Virgin Mary. Catherine was proclaimed a saint in July 1947.

La Salette (preceding pages): When the sun sets behind the mountains, the illuminated pilgrimage trail leads to the Basilica Notre-Dame-de-la-Salette. The burning candles and torches draw a giant letter 'M' at the foot of the sanctuary. Evening vigils there, which end with a procession round the site of the Virgin's appearance, are an unforgettable experience for the pilgrims who come to visit the Beautiful Lady. Since 1852, Saletine monks and nuns have been passing Her message on to all the five continents.

Paris: The Chapel of Revelations, nestling between Parisian houses, is always full of people who come with hope and often return, enchanted by the unusual atmosphere. They can pray before the reliquary containing the heart of Saint Vincent de Paul, and the sarcophagus of Saint Louise de Marillac. Ten years into his priesthood, under the influence of the time spent in ministry among the neglected peasants and convicts, Saint Vincent decided to dedicate his life to the poor. Saint Louise was an active supporter of this charitable work. Together, they founded the Sisters of Charity, whose 'convent is the sick-room, their chapel the parish church, their cloister the city streets'. At the time of her death in 1660, there were already over forty houses of the sisters in France, the sick and poor were looked after in twenty six Parisian parishes, hundreds of women were given shelter.

Paris: The interior of the chapel contains the statue of the Virgin Mary, made in accordance with Catherine Labouré's description of her vision. She saw the Mother of God, holding up the globe and offering it to God in a gesture of supplication. A moment later the globe had disappeared, and the Virgin lowered Her hands, from which rays of bright light began to emanate.

Paris: In this armchair, the Virgin Mary appeared to Saint Catherine Labouré. The Virgin said to the nun, who was kneeling at Her feet: 'Come before this altar. Anybody who prays fervently here, with hope in their heart, will be answered. Trust in me, and I will be with you.' More than a million and a half pilgrims visit the chapel every year.

Paris: The Medal has caused many miracles, recognised by the Church, and has helped numerous people to return to God. The rays of grace flow from the Virgin Mary's hands, and the text reads 'O Mary, conceived without sin, pray for us, who seek recourse in Thee.' The reverse shows the letter 'M' inscribed over the cross. Underneath there are two hearts: the one belonging to Jesus bears the crown of thorns, and His Mother's heart is struck through with a sword and encircled by roses. They are surrounded by twelve stars. The first 1,500 copies of the Miraculous Medal were minted in 1832, following the Virgin's wish, expressed to Sister Catherine. They quickly became a source of blessings. Particularly famous was the conversion of a Jewish banker, Alphonse Ratisbonne, who was offered the Miraculous Medal in Rome and accepted it.

Paris: Pilgrims from all over the world pray at rue du Bac for the Virgin Mary's intercession. Thousands of plaques left in the chapel's courtyard, express thanks to the Virgin, bearing testimony to the fact that many prayers have been answered.

Lourdes: In 1858, beginning on 11 February, the Mother of God appeared to Bernadette Soubirous on eighteen occasions. Bernadette was canonised in 1933. In the thirteenth vision, the Virgin said 'Tell the priests to build a chapel here.' The sanctuary near the Grotto of Revelations, famed for its miraculous healing properties, is visited every year by six million pilgrims.

Lourdes: The Grotto of Revelations under Massabielle (the White Rock) lies on the river Gave, at the foot of the Pyrenees. The first procession to the Grotto set off from Lourdes on 4 April 1864, two years after the Church commission proclaimed that 'the revelations show all signs of authenticity'.

Lourdes (preceding pages): Lourdes is the biggest centre of Marian worship in the world. Every evening, thousands of people with lit candles and paper lanterns walk in procession from the Gave embankment to the city, and then turn back towards the basilica. The sick and the disabled use wheelchairs and specially adapted beds to join in the procession.

Lourdes: The stone plinth of the statue was inscribed with the words 'I am the Immaculate Conception', spoken by the Mother of God when She appeared at Lourdes for the last time.

QUE SOY
ERA
IMMACULADA COUNCEPCIOU!

Lourdes: The documentation relating to over six thousand healings is kept in the archives. The Church confirmed the miraculous nature of seventy of them. Nobody can account, however, for the number of spiritual healings which occur here. The sick, even those who are gravely ill, are brought over to the Grotto. They are looked after by members of their own families or volunteers from many charitable bodies and associations of hospital workers which are active in France and other countries. Those people give their time freely in order to enable even those who cannot walk to visit the sanctuary dedicated to the Virgin Mary.

Lourdes: There are daily processions to Massabielle. The volunteers carrying a cross precede the sick and disabled who pray for their health to be restored. At Lourdes, one can feel the presence of Christ, as well as of the Virgin Mary. The Eucharastic processions and all-day vigils before the Holy Sacrament take place every day.

Lourdes: Everybody who visits Lourdes wants to come into direct contact with this miraculous place, if only for a moment. There is almost always a long queue of those who wait to touch or kiss the rock in the Grotto, chosen by the Virgin for Her meeting with Bernadette.

Lourdes: Those who seek hope and consolation, keep vigil and pray at the Grotto of Revelations. They know that here, as Pope John Paul II put it, 'the Virgin Mary, who is without sin, comes to the aid of sinners'.

Lourdes: It would be impossible to conceive of Lourdes without the praying crowds. Over half of the pilgrims arrive here from abroad. The sound of French mixes with German, Italian, English, Polish and Spanish. It is only when they all say 'Ave Maria' that the people's voices unite. They hold up their burning candles, just as Bernadette Soubirous used to do. The light spills like lava at the base of the Massabielle hill, where the holy Grotto is situated.

Lourdes: The procession of the sick and disabled makes its way to the Grotto. There is a long-standing tradition of their participation in pilgrimages to Lourdes. The first one was organised in 1873, which in the nineteenth century was not a simple matter. The first miraculous healing, recognised by the Church, occurred as early as the time of the thirteenth revelation: Catherine Latapie from the village of Loubajac regained movement in her arm, after dipping it in the water of the source which springs in the Grotto.

Lourdes (preceding pages): Every evening, after people have finished saying the rosary for the last time, they set off in procession. The burning candles throw their light on the pilgrims' faces, dispersing the darkness, encroaching like a sparkling wave, which stops in its tracks when the procession ends with a solemn *Salve Regina*.

Lourdes: The procession is heading for Saint Bernadette's Basilica. It is a modern church, which can accomodate five thousand believers. It was built at the site where Bernadette prayed during the last appearance of the Virgin Mary, after the Grotto had been closed by the police as a place of an illegal cult.

Lourdes: Pope John Paul II said here in 1983: 'Suffering is always a reality, a reality with a thousand faces.'

Lourdes: Care for the sick who arrive at Lourdes on pilgrimage is very well organised. There are several hospitals and hospices where they may be looked after for a few days. They can also bathe in the specially constructed pools, filled with the healing water. Afterwards, the disabled in their wheelchairs pray in the adjacent Grotto of Revelations.

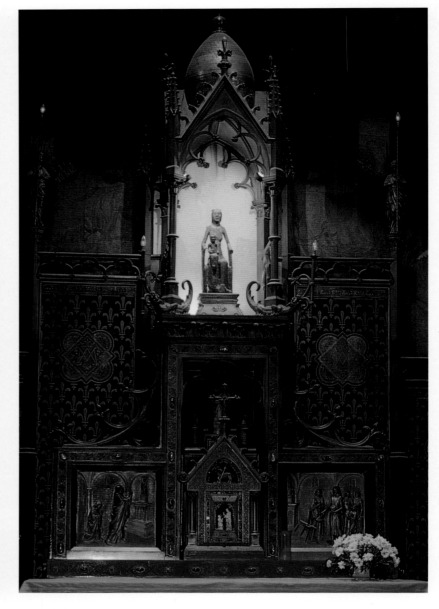

Rocamadour: Approaching Rocamadour from the valley of the Alzou river, one has the impression that this small medieval town, dominated by its church and the fortified castle walls, is clinging to a vertical rock, as if suspended half way between the earth and the sky. During the Middle Ages it was one of the most important places of Christian pilgrimages, on a par with the Holy Land, Rome and Santiago de Compostela.

Rocamadour: Two hundred and sixteen steps, called *Via Sancta,* lead to the Miraculous Chapel which houses the Romanesque wooden statue of the Virgin Mary with Child, sitting on the throne. Pilgrims used to ascend them on their knees. Under the vaulted ceiling hangs the iron bell which is considered to possess wonderous powers – it once tolled, warning the town of impending danger.

Rocamadour: The statue of the Mother of God is over a thousand years old. An annual retreat takes place before it between 8 and 15 September. Popes and French, English and Czech kings came to pray here.

Le Puy: In 1860 a statue of the Virgin Mary, cast from the cannons captured in the battle of Solferino in 1859, was erected on the rock known as Corneille. The statue, which dominates the Massif Central, is known as *Notre Dame de France* and is venerated as the Patron Saint of the country. Before the miracle at Lourdes, le Puy used to be the biggest Marian sanctuary in France. From here Pope Urban II set off for Clermont, where he called on Christians to free the Holy Places in Palestine from Muslim hands.

Le Puy: The Black Madonna, a Romanesque statue of the Virgin Mary with the Infant Jesus on Her lap was brought to France in 1254 by King Louis IX, otherwise known as Saint Louis, after one of his Crusades. During the French Revolution it was burned in the town square and today its exact copy can be seen in le Puy cathedral.

Le Puy: The statue of the Virgin Mary with the Infant Jesus is over forty two foot high. It is probably the only representation of the Virgin whose interior one can enter, like that of the Statue of Liberty in New York. From the top of the internal stairs, the view of the magnificent basilica and the town can be enjoyed through the little windows cut out in the metal cast.

Bétharram: The interior of the chapel consecrated by Bishop Lescar in 1661 strikes visitors with its solemn, restrained beauty.

Bétharram: The seventh station of the famous Way of the Cross is located on the hill over the seventeenh century church on the river Gave. It has been visited by pilgrims ever since the church was built.

Bétharram: The statue of the Mother of God was made in 1845 by Alexandre Renoir.

GREAT BRITAIN
IRELAND

GREAT BRITAIN IRELAND

Inhabitants of the British Isles and Ireland, made up of the English, Welsh, Scots and Irish, are usually described by outsiders as 'the islanders'. This term has many different connotations, depending on its historical, political and even psychological nature. Although continental Europe is only separated from the islands by a narrow strip of water, crossing the English Channel always had a symbolic significance. It was as much the case during the Roman conquests and in the days of William the Conqueror, as it is today. People who live here are characterised by an unusually strong need to be different than others, to have a strong sense of their own, unique identity.

Walsingham (left):

The wooden statue of the Mother of God with Infant Christ can be seen at the Catholic Slipper Chapel. The chapel, which was restored at the end of the nineteenth century, was proclaimed the English National Catholic Sanctuary in 1934. Twenty years later the statue was crowned with Papal crowns.

Walsingham (preceding pages):

Every year, on the Feast Day of the Birth of the Virgin Mary, the statue of Our Lady of Walshingham is carried for several miles in a procession which begins at the Slipper Chapel. Knights of the Holy Sepulchre and Knights of Malta carry the statue on their shoulders, and here the procession is led by the Archbishop of Westminster, the late Cardinal Basil Hume.

The proverbial 'splendid isolation' of the inhabitants of the British Isles is seen almost as a national characteristic, defining their mentality and behaviour. However, it proved to be no obstacle to creating an empire, over whose dominions, according to the often quoted words of Christopher North, 'the sun never sets'. The Empire used to be seen as a symbol of continuity and stability in the world of international politics. Great Britain was always at its heart, with a metropolis in London, and Greenwich as a point from which both longitude and time were measured throughout the world. The history of the British Empire conveys to a never-ending chronicle of colonial conquests, economic and financial expansion, advancement of the British way of life and, above all, of the English language. The spiritual aspect of history is invariably more elusive, so it is quite feasible that no school text or learned treatise mentions the fact that in 1897, after a gap of four centuries, the tradition of pilgrimages to Walsingham, the main Marian sanctuary in England, was revived. The date is significant not only for English Catholicism, but also for the Anglican community, which recognises the prominence of the Virgin Mary as well. Consequently, the dialogue between two traditions – apart from the initiatives undertaken at the highest level by both Churches, Catholic and Anglican – takes place on a local, but nevertheless very impotrant, level. After all, the worshippers meet at the feet of Mary.

Since King Henry VIII signed the Act of Supremacy in 1534, completely abolishing Papal authority and raising the king to be Supreme Head of the Church of England, Great Britain has been largely associated with the Reformation. This one-sided viewpoint ignores the magnificent heritage of English Catholicism, both at the time when it was a national religion and during the course of the last two centuries, when Cardinal Newman or G. K. Chesterton were among those influential thinkers who defined the new approach to questions of faith, close to the modern ways of thought.

The Act of Supremacy was preceded by nearly fourteen centuries of English Christianity, which

Walsingham: The famous arch near Walshingham is all that remains of the fourteenth century shrine church and Augustinian monastery. They were destroyed as part of the dissolution of monasteries and Henry VIII's drive against Papal power. Towards the end of the nineteenth century, after a gap of over four hundred years, the veneration of the Virgin Mary, a significant feature of English religious life in the Middle Ages, was revived again.

had a strong Marian element, given to it by King Alfred, and later confirmed by Richard II who offered his kingdom to the Virgin as Her 'dowry'. Afterwards, English kings ruled the country not in their own name, but as vassals of the Mother of God. Although the Reformation had swept away material expressions of the Virgin's presence – sanctuaries, statues and reliquaries which were destroyed in all parts of the realm – people who live in the British Isles have retained in their hearts the indelible memory that they are Her special inheritance. This memory continues to bear fruit in our day. The sanctuaries at Walsingham, Glastonbury and Aylesford, rebuilt from ruins, do not resemble the magnificent Gothic churches that they once were, none the less they are a manifestation of longing for a continuity with the days of one, single, undivided Church.

Małgorzata Rutkowska

Walsingham: A similar statue of the Mother of God can also be found in an Anglican church nearby, in a replica of the Loreto shrine. The original shrine was built in the eleventh century, at the Virgin Mary's wish.

Walsingham: Custom dictates that those participating in the procession, should attempt to touch the miraculous statue, if only for the briefest of moments. Around half a million pilgrims come here every year.

Walsingham: The Catholic Slipper Chapel and the Chapel of Reconciliation stand side-by-side. There is also the New Loreto Shrine, which contains a statue of the Mother of God, created to resemble the original one. The shrine belongs to the Anglican Church. Consequently, Walsingham is visited both by Catholics and Anglicans.

Walsingham: During the national pilgrimage to Walsingham, representatives of both traditions pray together near the Lone Arch, giving a practical demonstration of Ecumenism. Despite earlier reserve, relations between the two communities are becoming increasingly cordial.

Walsingham: The statue of the Mother of God is carried at the head of the procession. The participants include prominent Church dignitaries, with Cardinal Basil Hume among them.

Walsingham: The main celebrations at the Slipper Chapel always begin at noon. However, the faithful already start to arrive in the early hours of the morning, to prepare for the devotions in honour of the Virgin Mary by saying the rosary together. In this way, believers travelling from all over the country are united in veneration of the Virgin, regardless of their race, age and social background.

Walsingham: In the Middle Ages, this Norfolk town already equalled Rome and Jerusalem as a pilgrimage site. It was often visited by English monarchs. At the beginning of the sixteenth century Erasmus of Rotterdam came here on pilgrimage.

Walsingham: Pilgrims who gather at the feet of the Mother of God, are united by prayer and their rosaries. Followers of both traditions venerate the Virgin in their separate churches, only a short distance apart from each other.

Aylesford: History of this sanctuary goes back to the
thirteenth century and the Crusades. All that remains from
that time are traces of old buildings, bearing testimony
to the unhappy fate of the Carmelite friary over the centuries.
Nowadays the shrine has a stark modern look.

Aylesford: Pilgrims come here
to pray before the statue of the
Virgin Mary and the relics of Saint
Simon Stock. He was Prior General
of the Carmelite Order, who
consolidated its position, leading
to the establishment of several new
foundations, four of them
in university cities, Cambridge,
Oxford, Paris and Bologna.
According to tradition, in 1251
he experienced a vision of the
Virgin Mary, as a consequence of
which there arose what is known
as the 'Scapular devotion',
widespread among Roman
Catholics. Two well-known Latin
hymns to Mary are usually
attributed to his authorship.

Carfin: In 1922, the efforts of Canon T. Taylor, who had particular reverence for the Virgin Mary, were rewarded with the creation of a replica of the Lourdes Grotto in Carfin near Glasgow. It was built by unemployed miners. The sheer number of worshippers who came to visit, quickly turned the place into the leading sanctuary in Scotland dedicated to the Virgin.

Carfin: Evening prayers take place every night at the new chapel built of glass. The Lockerbie disaster occured during the construction. To commemorate its victims, the chapel was named after the stricken plane – Our Lady, the Sea Maiden.

Looking at the history of Ireland, one would be justified in thinking that the veneration of the Virgin Mary has survived there almost as a secret, shared by the Irish people. The Virgin was an extremely important part of many of their lives, but She was not ruling in splendour. The legends recall the amazing gift, given to Saint Ita for her life filled with sacrifice, work on behalf of others and love of Christ. She received nothing less than the right to look after little Jesus. From the hands of Mary – a mother, she accepted a child – God. There are a few mentions of the Virgin Mary in the first Irish poems, written as long ago as the fifth century. The ringing of a bell calling the hermits to prayer and the song of a bird which sang for the monks, contained a memory of Her, but these were fleeting moments, quick rays of light breaking through the clouds. There was nothing more, despite strong links of early Irish Christianity with traditions of the Eastern Church. The saints whose cult was widespread were above all Patrick, Columba and Kevin. Patrick's emblems are snakes and shamrock, and his writings show his great humility and determination to carry out God's work: 'I, Patrick a sinner, am the most ignorant and of least account among the faithful... I owe it to God's grace that so many people should through me be born again to Him'. Columba, equally revered in Ireland and Scotland, was said to be 'loving to every one, happy-faced, rejoicing in his innermost heart with the joy of the Holy Spirit'. Kevin on one occasion supposedly prayed for so long that a bird built a nest among his fingers, whereupon Kevin continued praying, until the little birds had grown and could leave the nest. As Saint Kevin used the words of the oldest Irish prayers, he would have invited Jesus, and obiviously the Virgin Mary as well, to his dwelling as welcome guests, just as they were once asked to attend the wedding at Cana.

Frequent invasions, in particular the worst persecution that the Irish Catholics had ever experienced, during the days of Cromwell, and the destruction left in its wake by his army, were not conducive to building churches. In more clement times, when oppression, expropriation and arrests

Knock: This is the national sanctuary of Ireland. Here, on 21 August 1879, the Mother of God appeared to eighteen inhabitants of the village.

ceased to be everyday occurences, all those who aspired to any official position had to take an oath, renouncing the Catholic veneration of the Virgin Mary. Most probably, prayers to the Mother of God, the vanishing poetry in Gaelic and the disappearing culture lived on among trusted friends. The biggest Marian sanctuary in Ireland is at Knock in County Mayo. The soil there is not very fertile, and rarely arouses the desire of conquerors. Consequently, like the whole of this barren stretch of land in western Ireland, the area becomes a refuge of the dispossessed. During one of the periods of struggle, known in Irish history as the 'land wars', on a rainy evening in 1879, Mary McLoughlin, who was passing by the parish church, saw something that initially seemed to be like a group of stone statues, unexpectedly erected in the churchyard. When she rushed back with her friend, Mary Byrne, they saw the figures floating in the air above the ground. Later, a lot of people described seeing the same thing. The Virgin Mary came joined by Saint Joseph and Saint John the Evangelist, as Lady of the Family in which Jesus, God and man, felt most at home during His life on Earth.

Ernest Bryll

Knock: Our Lady of Knock was seen in Ireland at the time of poor harvests and hunger. The vision lasted for over two hours. During that time the Virgin did not utter a single word.

Knock: About eight in the evening, a group of locals saw the image of the Virgin Mary by the wall of the parish church. Saint Joseph was standing on Her right, and Saint John the Evangelist on Her left. In the background there was an altar with a large cross, and the Lamb of God before it. Six weeks after the apparation, a commission of twenty priests decided that the testimony of eye-witnesses sounded believable.

Knock: A modern church was built in 1976 for the steadily growing number of pilgrims. It can accommodate fifteen thousand visitors, and was designed by Daithi Hanly.

Knock: The first recorded case of a miraculous healing occured ten days after the appearance of the vision, when a twelve year old girl who was deaf regained her hearing. As a result, many ill and disabled people started arriving at Knock. Healing properties are attributed to the gable wall of the church, against which the Virgin Mary was seen.

Knock: Custom suggests that one should walk once round the church, saying the rosary. The appearance of the Virgin Mary seemed to underline Her role as queen, leading people to the Eucharist.

Knock: In 1954, declared a Marian Year, the statue of the Virgin Mary at Knock was honoured with a crown by Pope Pius XII. In 1960 Pope John XXIII offered a magnificent wax candle – the traditional gift of Popes to Marian sanctuaries throughout the world. On 30 September 1979, the hundredth anniversary of the vision's appearance, Pope John Paul II came to Knock and raised the local church to the status of a basilica, known as the Basilica of The Virgin Mary, Queen of Ireland. He also brought the Mother of God a rose made of gold.

Knock: The news of the Virgin Mary's silent appearance at Knock quickly reached the whole of Ireland. The inhabitants of the country saw it as a consolation for their attachment to the Church during the cruel persecution of Catholics in the period between the fifteenth and seventeenth century. The first group of pilgrims visited Knock's parish church as early as March 1880. Gradually, the veneration of Our Lady of Knock spread beyond Ireland's borders, to the United States and Australia, where there are large communities of Irish immigrants.

Lady's Island: The staue of the Virgin Mary dominates the island in the midst of lakes and farmland.

Lady's Island: The church which is close to the statue of the Virgin, brings together in prayer those who come here on pilgrimage towards the end of summer.

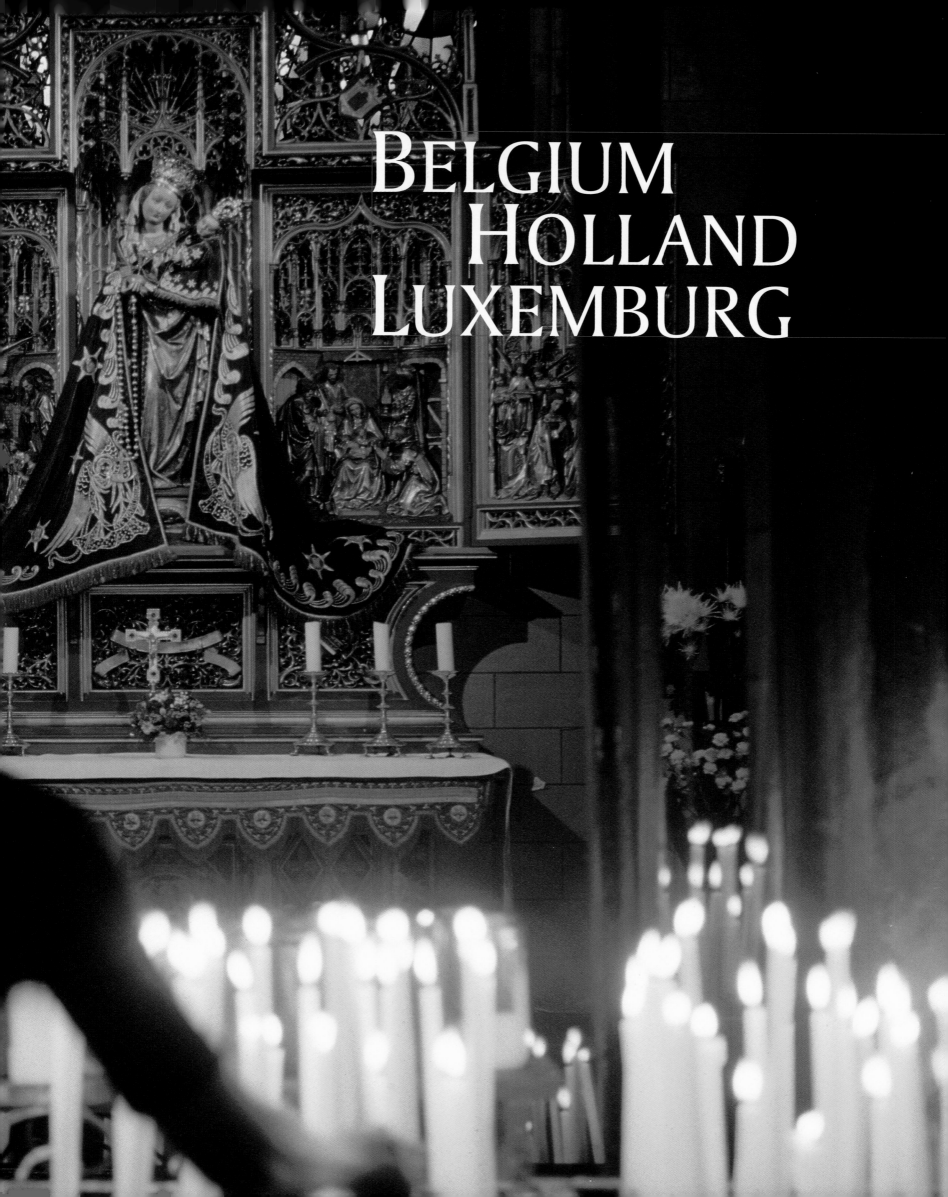

BELGIUM
HOLLAND
LUXEMBURG

BELGIUM
HOLLAND
LUXEMBURG

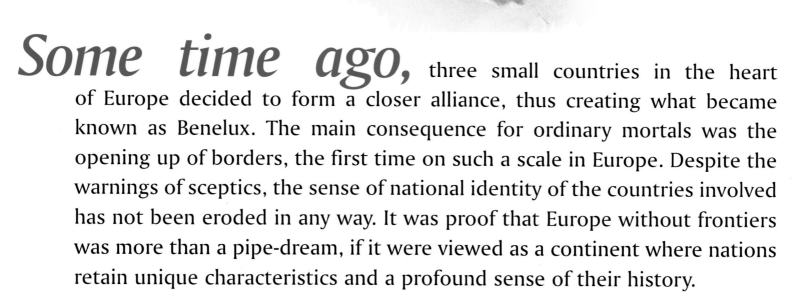

Some time ago, three small countries in the heart of Europe decided to form a closer alliance, thus creating what became known as Benelux. The main consequence for ordinary mortals was the opening up of borders, the first time on such a scale in Europe. Despite the warnings of sceptics, the sense of national identity of the countries involved has not been eroded in any way. It was proof that Europe without frontiers was more than a pipe-dream, if it were viewed as a continent where nations retain unique characteristics and a profound sense of their history.

Maastricht   (left):
The fourteenth century statue of the smiling Madonna, Star of the Sea, *Stella Maris*. When Protestants conquered the city in 1570, the miraculous statue was hidden in a Franciscan church. Between 1794 and 1804, during the French occupation, it was secreted in a private apartment. Later it was housed in the Church of Saint Nicholas. Finally, in 1837 it was moved to the Basilica of the Virgin Mary.

Maastricht   (preceding pages):
The statue of the Madonna in the twelfth century basilica has long been ascribed miracle-working powers. Ever since a man from Maastricht was miraculously saved from a disaster at sea when he invoked Her name, *Stella Maris* has been the Patron Saint of sailors. In 1912 Papal crowns were placed on the heads of the Virgin and Infant Christ, and on 5 September 1947 Dutch bishops performed an act of dedicating Holland to Her Immaculate Heart.

Belgium is a typical border country, which has always found itself in the sphere of influence of two different cultures – French and German. Over the centuries, their fusion has been reflected by unusual language divisions, officially sanctioned by laws passed in 1963, when the country was federalised. Modern Belgium consists of two large communities, which began to emerge in the early Middle Ages: French is spoken in Wallony and Flemish in Flanders, while Brussels is bilingual. As there was no common language and culture, Catholicism played the role of a unifying factor. The Church brought the Belgians together during their struggle for self-rule, and reinforced feelings of independence. Tradition contained elements which helped to define national identity, expressed in outstanding literature and art.

The region adopted Christianity between the third and fifth century, and through its spirituality and development of theological thought quickly made an impact on other Catholic countries. Its golden age began with the passing of Belgium into the hands of the dukes of Burgundy at the turn of the fifteenth century. Namur was the first place to celebrate *Corpus Christi*, the custom initiated by Saint Julianne of Mont Cornillon.

Reformation and religious wars of the sixteenth century broke up the Netherlands' spiritual and polictical unity. Whereas the Dutch managed to secure their independence at the time, the Belgians had to wait until 1830. Belgian Catholicism is characterised by the sincere piety of the common man, particularly evident in the Flemish part of the country, as well as the wide-spread practice of social and charitable work, numerous associations, unions and Catholic schools. One of the outstanding personalities of the Belgian Church was Cardinal Désiré-Joseph Mercier, a pioneer of Ecumenism in the first years of the twentieth century.

Belgium used to be referred to as 'the garden of the Virgin Mary', where She was the most beautiful rose of all. To this day, every region has at least one Marian sanctuary. Two of them have become known throughout Europe, as a result of the Mother of God appearing in both in 1933:

Sherpenheuvel (Montaigu): The statue of the Virgin Mary on the pinnacle of the roof of a church in Sherpenheuvel, the town whose name can be translated as a 'sharp pinnacle'.

Beauraing venerates her as the Refuge of Sinners, and Banneux, the Belgian Lourdes, as *Vierge des pauvres,* Mother of the Poor. Hanswijk near Malines, whose history goes back a thousand years, is justifiably proud of its miraculous Madonna statue from the Middle Ages. The statue's existence testifies to the continuity of Marian worship on Belgian territory. The national sanctuary at Hal, near Brussels, has undergone siege on several occasions, but never fell into the enemy's hands. This fact was attributed to the intercession of the Virgin Mary. Another statue of the Virgin which is greatly venerated can be seen at the seventeenth century sanctuary at Montaigu, visited annually by tutors and students from the local university at Leuven, who offer thanks for yet another successfully completed year of their studies.

Małgorzata Rutkowska

Banneux: This sanctuary at the French-German border was the location where in 1933 the Mother of God appeared to eleven year old Mariette Beco on eight separate occasions. Later, a centre of charitable work which encompasses the whole world was built, as well as a chapel near the family home of the Becos, the Institute of the Mother of the Poor, which cares for children, nine convents and monasteries, and a hospital.

Banneux: Dipping one's hand in the miraculous source of water and prayer in the Chapel of Revelations are part of tradition at Banneux. The poor, the ill and the heart-broken come here to seek solace, courage and hope. The Banneux Madonna is also the Patron Saint of the Romanies and circus artists, whose crowds arrived in 1985 to meet the Holy Father. Numerous statues, chapels and churches are dedicated to Our Lady of Banneux.

Beauraing: At the end of 1932 and beginning of 1933, in this Walloonian village in southern Belgium, the Virgin Mary appeared to a group of five children thirty three times. She repeated Her message from Fatima. Now She reigns in the chapel consecrated in 1954, the year Pope Pius XII created the Feast Day of the Virgin Mary, Queen of Heaven.

Beauraing: The statue of the Virgin Mary, Queen of Heaven, stands under a hawthorn tree, where the children experienced their visions. It was unveiled and blessed by the priests on 22 August 1946. More than 200,000 pilgrims from all over the world come here every year. The number of Her statues in the nearby Museum of the Virgin Mary exceeds a thousand, and there is also a collection of postal stamps with Her image.

Sherpenheuvel (Montaigu): In 1602, near the place where a miraculous statue of the Virgin Mary was found, Abbot Van Thienwinckel built for it a small chapel. Various indulgences were granted by Pope Pius V to those who came here on pilgrimage. On 25 August 1782 the statue was crowned. Nowadays it stands on the main altar of the church which was raised to the status of a minor basilica on 2 May 1922.

Sherpenheuvel (Montaigu): Several replicas of the statue of the Virgin were carved from the oak in whose branches the original statue had been found. These copies were given as a sign of respect to prominent people. The illuminated manuscript with the list of the recipients has survived.

Sherpenheuvel (Montaigu): In 1580, during the Reformation, the statue of the Virgin Mary was either stolen or destroyed. A faithful copy was made a few years later and can still be seen in the church at Sherpenheuvel. Over a million pilgrims visit the sanctuary every year. The numbers are paricularly high throughout May, and on 1 November, the Feast Day of All Saints. Quite often one encounters the tutors and students from nearby Louvain (Leeuven), the seat of the oldest Catholic university in Belgium.

The landscape of the Dutch plain is monotonous. The lie of the land causes land and water to merge into one. The land, painstakingly reclaimed from the sea, the fertile, flat fields known as polders, endless locks and canals are a testimony to Dutch people's success over the centuries in overcoming the limitations imposed on them by nature. At the same time, they have learned to utilise its gifts fully. This miniature country has proved to the world that the size of the territory is not a decisive factor in building a powerful state. Highly developed social and cultural structures and the ethos of hard work allowed Holland to play an important role in European economy and politics.

In the last few years one of the words which cropped up most often in the vocabulary of European politicians was Maastricht. This Dutch town near the Belgian border has become synonymous with discussions on European unity or lack of it since the 1992 Treaty defining the rules of partnership was signed there. In the heat of arguments about this document, the fact that Maastricht was also the birthplace of Dutch Catholicism and a symbol of its best traditions was often overlooked. Thanks to Maastricht's fourth century bishop, Saint Servatius, the country adopted Christianity. For hundreds of years, *Stella Maris*, the Star of the Sea, has been venerated in the Maastricht sanctuary. This proves the significance of Marian worship to Dutch Catholicism. A serious crisis within the Catholic Church in Holland, which first began in the 1960s and is manifested particularly in the internal disagreements among Catholics with regard to the Church's traditions and teaching, has not been an obstacle to many of them attempting to imitate the Virgin from Nazareth in their lives. The evidence can be found in Marian sanctuaries, of which there are many if one considers the size of Holland: 's-Hertogenbosch (Bois-le-Duc), Heiloo, Zegge, Aardenburg, Oostrum and Maastricht. Pilgrims come to all those places, to seek an answer to tormenting questions, born of contemporary Western civilization and the collapse of established values. Questions relating to the drama of human existence can be heard loud and clear in present day Holland. However, there are indications of the rebirth of the Dutch Church, which despite its difficulties has enriched the universal faith to a great degree, especially in the twentieth century, during the Second Vatican Council. Signs of hope that the current troubles can be resolved come also from Marian sanctuaries, where with Her words 'Do whatever He tells you to do' (Jn. 2:5), the Virgin Mary points out the way humanity must follow to reach God.

Małgorzata Rutkowska

's-Hertogenbosch: In the magnificent Gothic Cathedral of Saint John the Evangelist, with its five naves, the light of votive candles illuminates the statue of the Virgin Mary with the Infant Christ. It was found in 1380 during the work on enlarging the church. A year later, a woman named Hedwig, who had been paralised for three years, was miraculously cured. She used to pray often to the Gentle Mother of 's-Hertogenbosch. In 1382 a 'book of miracles' was placed in the cathedral. Its pages quickly filled with records of many miracles and special blessings.

's-Hertogenbosch: When Protestants took over the city in 1566, the miraculous statue had to leave the cathedral. It was kept in several locations, first in Antwerp, and later in Brussels, where it stayed for two hundred forty four years in the Church of Saint Jacob from Coudenberg, until it was finally returned to its rightful place in 1853. For centuries, even during the difficult days of the statue's absence, a traditional procession circling the town, known as *omgang*, took place on the first Sunday after the feast of the Annunciation. In 1903 Pope Leon XIII gave his permission to crown the statue.

LUXEMBURG

The Grand Duchy of Luxemburg, squeezed in between Belgium, France and Germany, has become one of the smallest countries in Europe. Life here runs its peaceful course, and the hereditary monarchy guarantees political stability. Extremely efficient financial institutions and profits from the tourist industry bring a high degree of prosperity.

By virtue of its loyalty to the Church of Rome and the Popes at the time of the Reformation and during the French Revolution, the Duchy of Luxemburg became known as the bastion of Christianity in this part of Europe. Christianity began to exert its influence here as early as the fourth century, but was fully accepted only at the turn of the seventh century, as a result of the apostolic activity of Saint Willibrord, an English missionary, who in about 700 established an important sanctuary at Echternach. He is still greatly venerated in Luxemburg, and his tomb at Echternach is visited by numerous pilgrims every 7 November, Saint Willibrord's Feast Day. In addition, on Whit Tuesday there takes place through the streets of Echternach and round the saint's tomb an hour's long processional dance of pilgrims, each group accompanied by its own brass band. This tradition has continued since before 1553, an unspoiled survival of ancient hallowed merry-making.

In 1666 the Mother of God, Help of the Afflicted, who covers those seeking Her help with Her cloak, was declared the Patron Saint of Luxemburg. In the words of Pope John Paul II's prayer during his visit to Luxemburg in 1985, the Virgin teaches 'the people the meaning of the affairs of the world, and love of the eternal'. Many towns and villages have Marian sanctuaries, attended by a high number of pilgrims. The little wooden statue of the Madonna in Vianden near the German border is known as the Help of the Sick. Our Lady of Miners reigns in Kayl. During the Reformation, the famous medieval sanctuary in Girst played the role of the main bastion of the Catholic faith.

After the Second World War, an impressive sanctuary of Christ the King and Our Lady of

Luxemburg: The statue of the Mother of God, Help of the Troubled, the Patron Saint of the Grand Duchy of Luxemburg, stands on the main altar of the Cathedral of the Blessed Virgin Mary. An official edict of 1666 put the Duchy into Her care. To commemorate this event, every year, between the third and fifth Sunday after Easter, the famous Extended Octave of Our Lady of Luxemburg is celebrated over fifteen days.

Fatima was built in Niederwiltz, in gratitude for freeing the country from German occupation. A magnificent stained glass window above the entrance to the cathedral in Luxemburg's capital was also intended as an expression of thanks for The Virgin's protection during the war. The inhabitants of Luxemburg fully understand that Her presence and help are needed by all.

Małgorzata Rutkowska

Luxemburg: During the Octave, the miraculous statue, dressed in elaborate garments, is carried in procession on a votive altar made in wrought iron by a craftsman from Luxemburg, Pierre Petit, in 1776. The statue is followed by representatives of the town's council, all the guilds and religious societies, as well as crowds of the faithful. In Her right hand, the Mother of God holds a sceptre, from which is suspended a gold key to the city gates, and to the hearts of its inhabitants.

MARIA MATER IESU

GERMANY
AUSTRIA
SWITZERLAND

GERMANY AUSTRIA SWITZERLAND

KEVELAER

PASSAU
ALTÖTTING

MARIAZELL

EINSIEDELN

MARIA SAAL

There is a general consensus that part of the German national character is the need to search for simplicity, clarity and synthesis, which may explain why Germany has produced so many outstanding philosophers and theologians. The same tendency led to the reforming movements within the Church, which gave birth to Protestantism. Although initially it triumphed among the German-speaking nations, Catholicism which had succeeded in retaining its ardour and commitment to faith, was gradually revived. This faith is expressed in many sanctuaries throughout Germany, Austria and Switzerland, where pilgrims continue to come in large numbers to venerate the Virgin.

Einsiedeln (left):
The sanctuary with the statue of the Virgin Mary stands at the site of a group of old hermitages, which were probably built in the ninth century.

Kevelaer (preceding pages):
There are many ways of going on pilgrimage. An unusual method has become popular in Kevelaer, near the German — Dutch border, where every year at the end of July and beginning of August, bikers on their shiny machines come to pay homage to the Virgin Mary.

Germany is a country that has achieved a rare feat of playing a pivotal role in European politics, economy and culture throughout most of its history. Its influence always reached far beyond geographical and political borders. Periods of harmonious co-operation alternated with dramatic incidents when Germany attempted to dominate other countries by means of military agression. In 843, as a result of the first partitioning of Charlemagne's empire, the kingdom of the Eastern Franks, under Louis the German, emerged as the nucleus of the German state. In 962, the aspirations of its rulers and drive for unity led to the creation of the Holy Roman Empire with the imperial coronation of Otto I. The First Reich lasted for nearly a thousand years, the Second – just under fifty, and the Third twelve years.

After the Second World War, Germany was divided into four zones, occupied separately by the victorious Allied Powers. Following the conflict between the Western Allies and the USSR, two separate German states were created in 1949. Berlin was eventually divided in 1961 by a wall, which became a symbol of the 'Iron Curtain' and the disposition imposed on Europe by the agreements of the Yalta Conference. Finally, the popular social movements of the 1980s changed the course of history. The Berlin Wall was torn down, and the Brandenburg Gate again connected the two halves of the city. The way lay open for the reunification of Germany and the slow process of healing the rifts within Europe.

Although Christianity has been present there for more than fifteen centuries, nowadays Germany is referred to mainly as 'the birthplace of the Reformation'. Martin Luther aimed only to strengthen and renew the Catholic Church, but instead succeeded in dividing Christianity into two factions: the north of the country chose Protestantism, the south remained Catholic. Today there are around three hundred Marian sanctuaries in Germany: some are small and visited mainly by local people, others have become internationally known. Most of them can be found in the sourthern regions of the country, particularly in Bavaria, where people's religious convictions

Kevelaer: The miraculous chapel stands at the centre of this small town, and all the main streets converge on it. The chapel was founded by Hendrick Busman, a local merchant who in 1641 was travelling from Cologne to Antwerp. He stopped by a wayside cross for a moment of prayer, and heard these words spoken by the Virgin Mary: 'Build a chapel for me at this site.' Over the next few days, they were repeated by Her on three more occasions.

manifest themselves in things like the customary greeting *'Grüss Gott'* (God be with you). The veneration of the Virgin Mary has always been one of the key elements of the German faith. Charlemagne carried a statue of the Virgin with him on every journey throughout his vast empire. In the Middle Ages the magnificent German cathedrals became an important destination for pilgrims. Most of them were dedicated to the Mother of God: in Aachen, Hildesheim, Cologne, Speyer, Reichenau and Ragensburg.

German Christianity still remains divided, but there is much evidence of a strong desire to build bridges. These tendencies have found support in the words of Pope John Paul II, who said during his visit to Germany in 1980: 'We cannot simply leave it at this: in that we are divided and always will be divided and at odds with each other.'

Małgorzata Rutkowska

Kevelaer: According to tradition, Busman's wife saw the chapel in her dreams, together with an icon of the Virgin. The couple searched for the icon, which turned out to be an engraving based on the image of Our Lady of Luxemburg. The tiny icon shows the Madonna with a sceptre in Her right hand, and carrying on Her left arm the Infant Christ, who is holding an orb representing the Earth. A view of Luxemburg stretches out in the background. In 1642 the icon was brought to the finished chapel, and soon began to attract crowds of believers. It became famous for miraculous healings and conversions to faith.

Kevelaer: The glow of candles in the Kevelaer sanctuary is seen as a visible form of prayer to the Virgin. Hundreds of them are lit in the famous Chapel of the Candles during Vespers, celebrated daily by the brotherhood known as *Consolatrix Afflictorum*. The sanctuary also contains the original chapel, built by the Busmans in 1654, the Chapel of Grace, the Neo-Gothic Basilica of the Assumption of the Virgin Mary, erected in 1864, and finally the modern chapel known as *Pax Christi*. Stations of the Cross were constructed on the outskirts of Kevelaer between 1889 and 1892. The three hundred foot high tower of the basilica dominates the sanctuary and the town.

Kevelaer: Initially the sanctuary of the Mother of God, Consoler of the Afflicted, attracted local people. Later, pilgrims from all over Germany and the Netherlands began to come. Since 1949, in the Chapel of Grace, a 'light of peace' has burnt continuously in front of the miraculous icon. The carved lamp holder is supported by three doves which represent Lourdes, Altötting and Kevelaer. All these places are dedicated to the Virgin Mary, Queen of Peace. Every Saturday morning a Mass is said there for world peace.

Kevelaer: The annual pilgrimage of bikers takes place on the third Saturday and Sunday in July. Several thousand motorcycles receive a special blessing from the priests. In accordance with tradition, the pilgrims bring candles to this sanctuary. The oldest among the surviving ones was given by pilgrims from Rees in 1643. On 2 May 1987 Pope John Paul II offered a votive candle, inscribed '*Totus Tuus*'.

Altötting: The historical documents are a testimony to the long-established tradition of veneration for the Virgin Mary – the Black Madonna. It has been part of religious life here since the days of Saint Rupert, known as the Apostle of Bavaria, who was active at the turn of the seventh century.

Altötting: This sanctuary is located at the heart of Bavaria, near the Alps. It houses twenty four urns containing the hearts of Bavarian rulers from the Wittelsbach dynasty, who bequeathed them to the Madonna in their wills.

Altötting: Around two thousand paintings, as well as votive plaques and crosses carrried round the sanctuary by pilgrims, are displayed here. In 1728 Pope Pius VI visited Altötting, whilst today over a million people come here every year.

Altötting: In 1623 Duke Maximilian I declared the Black Madonna the Patron Saint of Bavaria. The document, signed in his own blood, was placed at the feet of the Madonna, which is probably a copy of the original one from the days of Saint Rupert, and comes from the late thirteenth century. On Ash Wednesday and Holy Saturday, the elaborate garments are removed from it during the period of adoration.

Altötting: Every June members of a hunting fraternity
from Bavaria and Tyrol go on pilgrimage to the
Black Madonna. They wear traditional costumes and carry
the flags of their parishes. They also visit the Church of Saint
Anne and a Capuchin monastery, where for forty one years
a lay brother named Conrad was assigned to serve the
pilgrims. He died in 1894 and was canonised by Pope Pius
XI in 1934. The statue showing Saint Conrad of Parzham in
prayer can be seen at the Chapel of Grace, before the altar
with the miraculous statue of the Madonna.

Altötting: Many celebrations which draw on Bavarian folk traditions take place at the feet of the statue of the Virgin Mary. Some of the pilgrims are ill and disabled. They pray at the Chapel of Grace, where a miracle occurred in 1489, in which a drowned child came back to life.

Altötting: Since 1650 the faithful from the Upper Palatinate in Germany have been coming here on foot, in an annual pilgrimage to thank the Virgin for Her assistance during the religious wars, when Catholicism was preserved, and to renew the vows made at that time.

Passau: The sanctuary of Our Lady of Perpetual Succour stands near the German-Austrian border, where the Ilz and Inn rivers enter the Danube. The pilgrims ascend the long staircase on their knees. The sanctuary is looked after by the Capuchin Order.

Passau: The main altar contains the miraculous image of Our Lady of Passau. Emperor Leopold I placed before it the trophies won after a great battle on 12 September 1683, during the siege of Vienna by the Ottoman forces. Pope Innocent XI declared that the day of the Vienna victory would thereafter become the Feast Day of the Holy Name of Mary.

Passau: The image of Our Lady of Passau is a faithful copy of a painting by Lucas Cranach, a famous German painter at the turn of the fifteenth century. The chapel where it hangs is a favourite place for marriage ceremonies.

'You are the centre of this part of the world, like a strong heart' sing the Austrians about their homeland in the National Anthem. Austria is also quite often described as 'the heart of Europe' and 'a bridge between East and West'. These sentiments are no exaggeration, although the small country of today no longer resembles the vast Austro-Hungarian Empire of the Habsburgs. The unifying role it has always played in Europe, however, remains unchanged. Throughout different periods of history, the Austrian monarchy ruled over many nations, which varied widely in their culture and religion. The ability to bring together distinct civilizations is evident in Marian sanctuaries scattered all over the country, in particular the famous Mariazell, where German and Slavic pilgrims meet in united peace to this day. Maria Saal, Maria Plain in Salzburg and Maria Taferl at Marbes are also worth mentioning.

Christianity has been an important element of Austria's national identity ever since this former province of the Roman Empire adopted it at the turn of the seventh century. From the very beginning, the cult of the Virgin Mary had many followers and was particularly encouraged by monasteries and abbeys of the Benedictine and Cistersian Order. During the Reformation, Austria remained faithful to Rome and was seen as the bastion of Christianity, guarding Europe against the threat of the Ottoman expansion. The great victory of the combined armies of Catholic countries in the battle of Vienna in 1683 was attributed to the intercession of the Virgin. John III Sobieski, King of Poland, came to the rescue of the beleagured Austrian Emperor. His winged hussars dealt a decisive blow to the Grand Vizir's army. King John wrote to his wife: 'Untold spoils have fallen into our hands... There is powder and amunition alone for a million men... The Vizir took such hurried flight that he had time to escape with only one horse... I have all the tents, and cars, *et mille autres galanteries fort jolies et fort riches*...They left behind a mass of innocent Austrian people, particularly women; but they butchered as many as they could... The Vizir had

Mariazell: This quiet little village in Styria, picturesquely situated among the low Eastern Alps, and about hundred and twenty kilometres from Vienna, attracts pilgrims and skiers alike.

a marvellously beautiful ostrich... but this too he had killed... He had baths; he had gardens and fountains; rabbits and cats, and a parrot which kept flying about so that we could not catch it...' To commemorate the victory, Pope Innocent XI declared 12 September the Feast Day of the Holy Name of Mary, celebrated to this day by the Catholic Church throughout the world.

The First World War swept away the old Austro-Hungarian Empire. Austria, reduced to its original core territory, turned into a republic. After the last war, it was occupied by the Allied Powers. Freedom did not come until 1955. Many people associated it with the Rosary Crusade for Peace of a Franciscan monk, Father Peter Pavlicek. His idea was simple: 'If it is possible to gather millions of people in order to send them to war which will cause massive destruction, would it not be easier for us to get together and work on an Austrian peace initiative?'. Following the departure of the last units of the occupying army, Father Pavlicek was named a 'liberator'. Chancellor Julius Raab admitted that 'Prayer was Austria's weapon and her strength.'

Małgorzata Rutkowska

Maria Saal: This sanctuary was established by Saint Modest in the seventh century. In the Middle Ages, the rulers of Carinthia were crowned here. In 1425 a miraculous statue of the Madonna with Child arrived in the local church, probably from Italy. During the wars with the Ottoman Empire the sanctuary was damaged on many occasions. After the fire of 1669, the church was rebuilt and the addition of two tall towers made it more likely to withstand a siege.

Mariazell: The oldest Austrian sanctuary is one of the main pilgrimage sites in Central Europe. Over a million believers from Austria, Germany, Hungary and Slav countries visit it annually.

Mariazell: This statue of the Mother of God, famous for the blessings it bestows upon people, is made of limewood. It arrived at Mariazell in 1157, with a Benedictine monk called Magnus, who lived here as a hermit. He erected a small chapel resembling a cell in a monastery, and placed the statue inside. This was the origin of the name Mariazell, which means 'Maria's cell'. In 1200, the first church was built at the same site in the Romanesque style.

Mariazell: Our Lady of Mariazell – The Great Mother of Austria and the Slavic People, the Great Lady of the Hungarian People, was crowned in 1908. The Hungarian King Louis I the Great, father of Saint Hedwig, in gratitude for a victory over the Turks founded a Chapel of Grace in the new, Gothic church. The miraculous statue was placed there. Between 1644 and 1704 the church was remodelled in the Baroque style. In the seventeenth century Mariazell became the main sanctuary of the whole Habsburg Empire.

Mariazell: Outstanding agriculturalists and farmers who came here on pilgrimage, are being given commemorative plaques with an image of the Great Mother of Austria. In 1339 Pope Boniface IX issued a bull granting privileges to the sanctuary, among others a chance for pilgrims to receive plenary indulgence. Chronicles note that at the beginning of the sixteenth century pilgrims came to Mariazell from almost every country in Europe.

Mariazell: The courtyard in front of the church is the meeting place for pilgrims arriving here from all over Austria. In centuries past, Mariazell was visited by almost all the rulers of Austria from the Habsburg dynasty. Empress Maria Theresa received her First Communion here, and in dangerous moments of history crowds walked in procession and prayed 'O Mother of God, protect the Holy Roman Empire and all its people!'

Mariazell: During the main celebrations of the Feast Days of the Assumption and the Birth of the Virgin Mary, the interior of the basilica fills up with standard bearers who arrive here at the head of various pilgrim groups from Austria and neighbouring countries. The tradition of pilgrims walking on foot all the way from Vienna to Mariazell was revived in the 1980s.

Mariazell: Mariazell is also a tourist attraction and a lively centre of cultural life, where musical traditions in particular are carefully maintained. The treasury has a magnificent collection of works of art, where pilgrims can admire liturgical accessories, portraits, carvings and statues made of cedar wood, marble and ivory.

SWITZERLAND

Unity in multiplicity is one of the main characteristics of Switzerland. In 1291 three cantons decided to assert their political independence from the German Empire and formed an 'Everlasting League' of self-defence. They were Schwyz, from which the country's name, *die Schweiz,* is derived; Uri and Unterwalden. The legendary hero of this event is William Tell. Gradually the original three cantons were joined by other likeminded districts. At present Switzerland consists of twenty three cantons and half cantons, administered by separate authorities. German, French, Italian and Romansh are the national languages. In the circumstances, one could justifiably ask what do the inhabitants of the Swiss Confederation have in common. There are several possible answers: their shared history, deeply embedded love of freedom, and traditional values, such as tolerance, hospitality and hard work. The Swiss are in the habit of saying 'We do not have any natural resources, our wealth comes from work.' Indeed, those who admire the standard of living in Switzerland, often forget the efforts of many generations which were necessary to achieve it. Almost two centuries ago Switzerland chose neutrality as a path to political and economic success. Combined with democracy, it meant that this tiny country became the banking centre of Europe and the world.

The awareness of unwritten laws governing assistance to those affected by various misfortunes and of the need for peaceful co-existence are part of the Swiss ethos. Consequently, it was to be expected that the international community would settle on Geneva as the home of the League of Nations during the inter-war period, while nowadays several sections of the United Nations and the International Labour Organisation are housed there. The International Committee of the Red Cross also resides in Geneva, and this more than anything else testifies to the Swiss empathy with human suffering. This attitude is equally evident in the country's religious and spiritual life. Geneva was also chosen for the headquarters of the World Council of Churches, which represents

Einsiedeln: A Benedictine monastery, located at the tectonic foreland of the Alps, at nearly three thousand feet above sea level, is the most significant of the Marian sanctuaries in Switzerland. Swiss farmers and shepherds hold their religious meetings here. At the beginning of the Mass they blow the alpenhorns, a characteristic instrument of the mountain regions.

around three hundred Christian Churches, and this fact takes on a symbolic significance.

The veneration of the Virgin Mary was very much in evidence in Switzerland during the Middle Ages. In the fifteenth century all the church bells were embellished with Her image together with a fragment of the text of the 'Angelus', in the hope that this would secure the Virgin's protection for wherever the ringing of those bells could be heard. Apart from the main sanctuary in Einsiedeln, there are Marian shrines in all regions of the country, with the Italian-speaking part priding itself on the statue of the Madonna del Sasso in Locarno, the German speakers venerating the icon of the Mother of God of Consolation in Mariastein, and the French going on pilgrimages to the sanctuary of the Blessed Virgin Mary in Lausanne.

Małgorzata Rutkowska

Einsiedeln: The Black Madonna, a copy of the Romanesque statue destroyed in the fire of 1465, stands in the Chapel of Grace, built at the site where the original was placed by Saint Meinard in the ninth century. The veneration of the Virgin began here after Saint Meinard was murdered by robbers in 861. Being a holy man, he was regarded as a martyr. A succession of hermits occupied his hermitage, which is what the name Einsiedeln means, and eventually a proper Benedictine monastery was established there.

Einsiedeln: The Baroque basilica
was erected between 1719 and 1735.
As early as the fourteenth century,
pilgrims began to arrive at Einsiedeln
from all over Switzerland, Austria
and Germany. It was also a starting
point for pilgrimages to the tomb
of Saint James the Great at Santiago
de Compostela in Spain.

Einsiedeln: The miraculous statue
of the Madonna has been on the same
site since the ninth century and is now
enclosed by the Chapel of Grace,
constructed of black marble. Following
a long-standing tradition, Swiss cantons
bring votive beeswax candles as an
offering to the Black Madonna. In 1934
the statue was crowned by the
Archbishop of Milano, Cardinal Schuster.

Einsiedeln: The interior of the sanctuary of the Black
Madonna is an outstanding example of Baroque architecture.
The revolutionary French army looted and badly damaged
the Chapel of Grace, but the statue survived, hidden
by one of the monks. The Benedictine Friars returned to the
monastery in 1801, and between 1815 and 1817 restored
the chapel and placed the statue there once more.

Einsiedeln: Traditional, colourful parades take place in the courtyard in front of the sanctuary. The Baroque monastery, built on a rectangle, was erected between 1704 and 1718. The Diorama of the Nativity and the View of Christ's Crucifixion can be seen nearby.

Einsiedeln: The sanctuary here is an important religious and cultural centre, attracting over half a million pilgrims every year. They come not only from Switzerland, but also from Germany, Austria, France, Italy, the United States and even Japan. The main celebrations take place on the Feast Days of the Ascension, *Corpus Christi,* The Assumption of the Virgin Mary and Our Lady of Einsiedeln, with the latter occuring on 16 July. The rosary procession on the first Sunday of October closes the annual pilgrimage cycle.

Einsiedeln: On 14 September, the day of the so-called 'angel blessing', established to commemorate the consecration of the church building in 948, the sanctuary is traditionally visited by mounted pilgrims. Colourful parades of people dressed in historical costumes pass through the streets. Over the centuries, many saints from various parts of Europe came to Einsiedeln. Among others they were Dorothy of Mątowy in Poland, Charles Borromeo from Italy and Peter Canisius, who was born in Holland but spent most of his life in Germany and died at Fribourg in Switzerland.

Einsiedeln: A priest departs after blessing the riders and their horses. At sunset, the pilgrims can hear the magnificent rendition of *Salve Regina* by the monks' choir. The Benedictines from Einsiedeln established many abbeys in the Schwyz canton during the Middle Ages.

ITALY
MALTA
SLOVENIA
CROATIA
BOSNIA
HERCEGOVINA

ITALY MALTA SLOVENIA CROATIA BOSNIA HERCEGOVINA

OROPA
PTUJSKA GORA
PADUA
BREZJE
MARIJA BISTRICA
VENICE
TRSAT
RAVENNA
FLORENCE
SINJ
LORETO
MEDJUGORJE
ROME
MENTORELLA
DEL DIVINO AMORE
SYRACUSE
TA'PINU
MELLIEHA
LA VALLETTA
MOSTA

The Adriatic, one of the most beautiful seas in existence, with an extremely picturesque coastline, has always separated the Appenine Peninsula from the Balkans. Although new intellectual and religious ideas travelled across to it from Italy, from the very beginning they met with the resistance of both the Eastern Church and Islam. The followers of the Catholic faith, members of the Orthodox Church and Muslims, had to live together on a relatively small territory, so peace came here rarely, and blood was shed on many occasions. Perhaps for this reason the Virgin Mary chose to appear at Medjugorje, to urge reconciliation and mutual forgiveness.

Loreto (left):
The cramped interior of the shrine has housed the statue of the Mother of God since the sixteenth century. After his victory at Vienna, King John III Sobieski of Poland gave the tent of the vanquished Grand Vizier to the sanctuary. The richly embellished cloth was used to make a canopy and vestments for the statue.

Loreto (preceding pages):
There are many ways of paying homage to the Virgin Mary. Here, Italian fighter planes leave a *tricolore* (the national colours of Italy) trailing over the sanctuary of Loreto.

Italy is a land of the Virgin Mary, and the veneration of Her has always been one of the most important ingredients of its religious life. There is no region where a Marian sanctuary cannot be found, or a town without a church dedicated to Her, and no village or hamlet, however small, without at least one simple roadside shrine containing Her image. Since the early days of Christianity, the Mother of God has been accorded great love and respect here. The most important symbol of this is the tomb of the Apostle Peter, the first Bishop of Rome, located under the Papal Altar in Saint Peter's Basilica. On one of its walls there are inscriptions from the third and beginning of the fourth century, where the name of the Virgin is visible next to those of Christ and Peter. Similar inscriptions of Her name, dating back to the third century, were also discovered in the Roman catacombs of Priscilla, together with frescoes containing scenes of the Annunciation and the Adoration of the Magi. Among the first temples built by the Christians after they had gained religious freedom as a result of the Edict of Milan, were two basilicas, dedicated to the Virgin Mary: Mother of God on Trastevere, and Saint Mary Major. The people of Rome erected many shrines with an icon or statue of the Virgin, known as *edicole*. Popes designated certain dates as Marian feast days and organised ceremonial processions in the Virgin's honour. The devotion to the Mother of God spread from Papal Rome to the rest of the Appenine Peninsula. Sicily was one of the first regions to be evangelised by Christians arriving here from the Near East. According to legend, in 42 A.D. Messina sent its envoys to Jerusalem, to pay homage to the Virgin. They brought back a letter saying *'vos et ipsam civitatem benedicimus'* ('I bestow my blessing upon you and your town.') These words were put on the plinth of the Virgin Mary's statue at the port. In Piedmont the first churches dedicated to the Virgin were founded by Saint Eusebius of Vercelli, who is presumed to have established the sanctuary at Oropa. Saint Maximus, his

Loreto: The Holy House of Nazareth has been venerated since the earliest days of Christianity. When Muslims took over the Holy Land, it was secretly taken apart and brought to Loreto via Dalmatia. The ancient inscriptions have survived on its walls. The earliest mention of the Holy House comes from 1294, when Angelo Niceforo made a gift of it to his daughter Tamara.

disciple and the first Bishop of Turin, placed a Byzantine icon of the Mother of God in the Church of Saint Andrew, laying a foundation for the cult of the Madonna known as *la Consolata,* which continues to this day. The magnificent Romanesque cathedral in Pisa is dedicated to the Mother of God Assumed into Heaven, and for many centuries all the ships, standards and coins of Pisa bore a legend *'Protege, Virgo, Pisas'* ('O, Virgin Mary, protect Pisa'). The first Marian church in Venice was built in 452. The greatest Italian poet, Dante Alighieri, celebrated the Mother of God in his verse, and all the Florentine painters of the Middle Ages and Renaissance depicted Her image: Cimabue, Duccio, Giotto, Simone Martini, Fra Angelico, Filippo Lippi and Sandro Boticelli. The Virgin was simply referred to as *Mia Donna* (My Lady), which led to the term Madonna.

Włodzimierz Rędzioch

Loreto: *'Ave Maria'* – a small child held by his mother salutes the miraculous statue of the Virgin Mary of Loreto. From the sixteenth century, the statue of the Virgin Mary from Loreto had been kept in the House of Nazareth. It was destroyed by a fire there in 1921. A year later a faithful copy of it was made.

Loreto: The Virgin Mary of Loreto is the Patron Saint of pilots, probably on account of a legend about the way the Nazareth house was brought over to Loreto by the angels. Every year, on National Aviation Day, Italian pilots travel to Loreto in great numbers, to pray before the statue. Before the first flight to the Moon in 1969, Neil Armstrong prayed at Loreto. After completing his mission, he placed a stone from the Moon's surface at the foot of the statue, in gratitude for his safe return.

Loreto: The construction work on the basilica began in 1469, during the pontificate of Pope Paul II. The Nazareth House, which until then stood in an open space, was enclosed by its walls on all sides.

Loreto: According to legend, angels were supposed to have
carried the house of the Holy Family over land and sea,
from Nazareth to the central Italian province of Ancona
in 1295 and placed it in a laurel grove. This *Casa Santa*
in the laurel grove (*lauretum* in Latin, hence Loreto)
became one of the most important pilgrimage shrines
in Christendom. Copies of it were built in several countries.
Over the centuries, thousands of pilgrims, kings and saints
among them, have travelled to the House of Nazareth,
in order to see the Madonna. Being able to say a rosary
here is a unique and memorable experience.

Loreto: The sanctuary of the Holy House is famed for numerous miracles, which have been attracting believers for many centuries. There is a clearly visible hollow in the marble step, where their knees have worn the marble away. The step forms part of the architectural and sculptural decoration surrounding the House, created by Bramante and other artists and craftsmen.

Loreto: The legend says that the three-walled Holy House, which was built underneath a rock in Nazareth, and where the Annunciation took place, was transported to Loreto by the angels.

Mentorella: The sanctuary of *Madre delle Grazie* (Mother of Grace), to the south of Rome, stands in the breathtakingly beautiful scenery of the Prestini Mountains. It is one of the oldest Marian sanctuaries in Italy, and was probably built in the early days of Christianity. This secluded spot which resembles a hermitage, situated on top of the Guadaguolo Mountain, was Cardinal Karol Wojtyła's favourite place to stay during his trips to Italy. It was also his choice for the first pilgrimage as Pope John Paul II, thirteen days after election to the Holy See on 29 October, 1978.

Mentorella: Famed for many blessings it has bestowed upon the faithful, this thirteenth century wooden statue can be seen in the Church of the Madonna della Mentorella. According to tradition, it was founded by the Emperor Constantine the Great.

The Vatican: An old fresco of the Virgin Mary, venerated as *Mater Ecclesiae*, Mother of the Church, has survived in Saint Peter's Basilica. On the instructions of Pope John Paul II, a copy of the fresco was painted on the facade of the side wing of the Apostolic Palace. It now looks over Saint Peter's Square. The Pope's coat of arms and his motto, '*Totus Tuus*' (All Thine), were added underneath the Virgin's image.

The Vatican: Devotion to the Virgin Mary spread to the whole of the Appenine Peninsula from Saint Peter's Square in Rome. The obelisque was brought to Rome in 36 A.D., and in 1586 it was placed at the spot where it now stands. It is said that it marks the place where the first Bishop of Rome died a martyr's death.

The Vatican: In 1580 Pope Gregory XIII had the fresco of Our Lady of Perpetual Succour moved from the old Saint Peter's Basilica to the chapel that bore his name in the present one. It was placed above the altar containing the relics of Saint Gregory of Nazianus.

The Vatican: The tomb of the Apostle Peter is sited at the very heart of the basilica dedicated to his name, under the Papal Altar. The name of the Virgin Mary is inscribed on the tomb's wall, beside those of Christ and Saint Peter. The inscriptions date back to the end of the third and beginning of the fourth century.

Rome: The Basilica of Our Lady of the Snows. In the middle of a hot summer in 352, on the night of 4 August, snow fell on one of the Roman hills, the Esquiline. The people of Rome were highly agitated by this miracle, and in order to commemorate it, Pope Liberius had a church built and dedicated to the Virgin Mary. Following the proclamation of the dogma of Mary as Mother of God, *Theotokos,* during the Epesus Council in 431, Pope Sixtus III erected an impressive basilica, which has survived to our times, although it was remodelled on several occasions. In recognition of its importance among churches dedicated to the Mother of God, the adjective *maggiore,* or major, was later added to its name.

Rome: According to legend, Saint Luke was supposed to be the creator of this ancient icon representing the Mother of God, *Salus Populi Romani* (The Salvation of the Roman People). It was said that he painted it during the Blessed Virgin's lifetime. Copies of this image can be found all over the world.

Rome: The *Salus Populi Romani* icon is displayed at the beautiful and highly ornate Borghese Chapel in the Basilica of the Virgin Mary of the Snows, built on the orders of Pope Paul V between 1611 and 1615.

Rome: On 5 August, the anniversary of when the miraculous snow fell, the Feast of the Virgin Mary of the Snows is celebrated at the basilica of Her name. White flower petals are scattered throughout the place.

Rome: During a celebratory Mass at the Basilica of Our Lady of the Snows, *Santa Maria ad Nives,* all the participants are trying to get hold of at least a few flower petals and take them home.

Rome: White flower petals are falling from the ceiling onto the Basilica of the Virgin Mary of the Snows during annual celebrations.

Del Divino Amore: About eight miles down the ancient road known as via Adreatina, in the thirteenth century the Orsini family built a fortified castle, called Castel di Leva. One of its towers was decorated with a fresco which showed the Virgin Mary with Child, and a dove, symbolising the Holy Spirit, flying above them. After the life of a pilgrim travelling through the area was miraculously spared, a church was built on the ruins of the castle and the fresco was transferred there.

Del Divino Amore: Every Saturday between Easter and the end of October, a midnight procession sets off from the Axum Obelischi at the Circo Massimo near the Forum Romanum. It follows the route along via Appia Antica and via Ardeatina to the sanctuary of *Madonna del Divino Amore,* the Patron Saint of Rome. The veneration for Her increased further after 1944, as the inhabitants of Rome believed that She saved the city from destruction.

Ravenna: In 1110, at the moment of the death of anti-Pope Clement III, a large marble carving appeared miraculously on the beach near the city. It showed a standing female figure, with her arms raised. There were eleven gold crosses decorating the veil and gown, and two medallions on the left and right of the figure's head. The Greek letters on the medallions made up the words 'Mother of God'. Peter from the Onesti family, a saintly monk from Ravenna, brought the carving to town and placed it in a little Church of Santa Maria. Since that day, 8 April, crowds of believers have been coming on pilgrimage to see the Greek Madonna. In the sixteenth century, work began on the church where the carving was finally moved.

Venice: The Venetians hold the Madonna in particularly high esteem. There are more than a dozen representations of Her in the Basilica di San Marco, the most important church in the city.

Venice: Travelling in a gondola along the Canale Grande or other, smaller canals, on both sides one sees the shrines dedicated to the Virgin Mary on the walls of the palaces and houses.

Venice: In 1204 Dodge Henrico Dandolo brought to Venice an icon captured during the Fourth Crusade. It was given the name of *Nicopeia* – The Mother of God in Glory. The painting was placed on one of the altars at the Basilica of Saint Mark. The inhabitants of the city declared Her the protectress of Venice. The image was carried in procession on Marian feast days and at times when Venice was under threat.

Oropa: The oldest surviving parts of the sanctuary date back to the thirteenth century, but most of the monumental buildings, positioned on a hillside, were erected in the Baroque style during the seventeenth and eighteenth century. In the twentieth century the so-called New Church was built above the sanctuary and covered with a large dome.

Padua: Following the tradition established by the Carmelites, the Madonna from the Basilica of the Blessed Virgin Mary on Mount Carmel was highly venerated. The devotion to Her was revived during a cholera epidemic at the end of the sixteenth century. It stopped after prayers had been said to the Mother of God. As an expression of gratitude, a statue of the Madonna, known as *Madonna dei Lumini*, the Madonna of Lights, or di Stefano dell'Arzere, was placed in one of the chapels of the church.

Padua: The Basilica of the Blessed Virgin Mary was erected on Mount Carmel. In 1309 the Carmelites began to build a church in the quarter of Padua known as *Molino* – the Mill. In 1491, an earthquake destroyed parts of the Gothic building, which was restored in the Renaissance style. The people of Padua have retained their respect for the Blessed Virgin of Mount Carmel, and every year organise a solemn procession on 16 July, the day when She is remembered in the Liturgy of the feast.

Oropa: In the mountains of Piedmont, in a Marian sanctuary above the town of Biella, which according to tradition was built on the instructions of Saint Eusebius of Torcelli, the statue of the Virgin Mary with Infant Christ brought over from Jerusalem is particularly venerated.

Florence: Among many Florentine churches devoted to the Virgin Mary the most famous one is the sanctuary *Santissima Annunziata* – the Most Holy Annunciation, built in the thirteenth century. It was remodelled by Michelozzo in the fifteenth century, and during the seventeenth a portico was added.

Florence: A breathtakingly beautiful fresco, which probably dates back to the beginning of the fourteenth century, can be seen at the Church of the Annunciation. It was created by an anonymous painter of the Florentine school, and shows the angel announcing to the Virgin Mary that She would be the Mother of the coming Messiah. According to legend, the painter fell asleep while working on the Madonna's head, and meanwhile an angel miraculously completed the image.

Syracuse: The greatest celebrations in honour of the Virgin Mary take place here on the anniversary of the first time that the tears appeared on the statue's face. The reliquary containing the tears of the Blessed Virgin is carried in procession from the home of the Janusso family, where the miracle occured, to the basilica.

Syracuse: 'Tears shed by the Madonna were tears of suffering, tears of prayer, tears of hope', said John Paul II on 6 November 1994, during his visit to a new, soaring church building in Syracuse, where the image of the Crying Madonna was placed.

Syracuse: The miraculous image of the Crying Madonna made from majolica used to belong to a married couple whose name was Jannuso. Hundreds of similar statues can be bought at any local shop dealing in devotional articles. Starting on 29 August 1953, for four consecutive days tears began to flow from the Madonna's eyes. They were subjected to scrupulous tests by scientists, who proclaimed them to be human. This led to the birth of the veneration of Our Lady of Syracuse, which increased further when numerous miracles and miraculous cures occured before Her image.

The Republic of Malta consists of four small islands in the Mediterranean. Its ancient name was Melita. It belonged successively to the Phoenicians, Greeks, Carthaginians, Romans and Saracens. For centuries it was part of the Roman Empire, and it was under its rule that Saint Paul established the first Christian community on Malta. After two years as a prisoner of the Romans in Jerusalem, the Apostle appealed for a trial at the emperor's court, and was sent to Rome, but he was shipwrecked at Malta. He stayed there for three months, spreading the word about the Son of God 'born of a woman' (Gal. 4:4) among the hospitable inhabitants of the islands. The veneration of the Mother of God began at the time of Malta's evangelization and despite the turbulent history of the place, it has survived to this day. The Saracens took over Malta in 870, and circa 1090 it was occupied by the Normans of Sicily. In 1530 the Habsburg Charles V granted Malta to the Joannites, who subsequently became known as the Knights of Malta. In 1565 the Muslims attempted to take over the islands once more. Two hundred Ottoman ships supported by pirates laid siege to Malta. The whole Christian world prayed for Malta's deliverance, and the enemy was repulsed on 7 September, the eve of the Feast of the Virgin Mary's Birth. Ever since then 8 September has been celebrated on the islands as a Marian Feast and Malta's National Day.

Apart from the sanctuary of Our Lady of Victories in Senglea, where the famous icon of the Damascene Madonna brought over from the Holy Land by the Joannites is venerated, the most important shrine is Ta'Pinu on Gozo, erected on the site of a sixteenth century chapel dedicated to the Virgin Mary, Ta'Gentili.

The oldest Marian sanctuary in Malta, Mellieha, stands on the northern coast of the main island itself. According to tradition, a monastery existed there as early as the fifth century. It was run by monks who followed the rule similar to the one laid down by Saint Augustine. This may be the reason why in 1584 the sanctuary was placed in the care of the Augustinian Order. At the centre

Gozo: Basilica Ta'Pinu on the island of Gozo is the national sanctuary of Malta. Built of local limestone, it blends in with the landscape.

of it there was a grotto with a fresco showing the Virgin Mary with Child. The ancient image was restored and crowned in 1899. The nineteenth century saw a new sanctuary of the Mother of God built in Mosta. The church was covered with a gigantic dome, whose diameter is over one hundred and thirty feet – one of the largest domes in the world.

There are around hundred and forty sanctuaries, churches and chapels on Malta dedicated to the Virgin Mary. Spiritual life there is very lively and full of conviction, and every Marian feast day turns into a popular celebration, with processions and fairs. Consequently, it would not be an exaggeration to call Malta 'the Archipelago of the Virgin Mary'.

Włodzimierz Rędzioch

Gozo: The miraculous painting of the Mother of God Assumed is among the most venerated of Her images in Malta. It was painted in 1619 by an Italian, Amadeo Perugino. In 1883 a local peasant woman, Carmela Grima, saw a vision of the Virgin here, which turned the icon into an object of veneration and pilgrimages. A large sanctuary was built in 1931, and the old chapel containing the painting, which was crowned in 1935, is its most important part.

Mellieha: The oldest Marian sanctuary in Malta, standing over the Bay of Saint Paul, consists of a stone church attached to the grotto with the miraculous image of the Virgin Mary on its wall. The ship carrying prisoners, among whom was Saint Paul, the Apostle of the Gentiles, was shipwrecked in Malta in the year 60 A. D. The passengers made their way to the island, which today bears Saint Paul's name. The grotto in Mellieha is supposed to have been the place where Saint Paul dwelt during his three month stay on the island. Nowadays the clothes of babies whose health was miraculously restored are displayed there.

Mellieha: The two votive paintings dating from the nineteenth century are typical of many such works, commemorating deliverance from disasters at sea and miraculous healings at the hospital run by the Knights of Malta. Pilgrims who are offered medical care there do not have to pay for it. For reasons of hygiene, every patient at the hospital used to be given silver dishes for his sole use.

Mellieha: In the depths of the large grotto which now forms part of the sanctuary there is an eleventh century fresco of the Virgin Mary with Child, famous for the blessings it has bestowed upon the faithful. The image remained undamaged during the Ottoman siege of 1565. During the seventeenth century the sanctuary was repeatedly threatened by pirate ships, but local people always guarded the fresco zealously. In 1587 Bishop Gargallo instructed the Augustinians to repaint it. In 1899 a crown was placed on the Virgin's head.

La Valletta: The Knights of Malta settled in the capital city in 1530. The town's name is derived from the Grand Master of those days, Jean de la Vallette. The order's symbol, the eight-point Maltese cross represents eight countries of the twelfth century Europe: England, the Kingdom of Aragon, France, Castille, Provence, Germany, Auvergne and Italy.

La Valletta: Madonna di Caraffa has found shelter in the Cathedral of Saint John the Evangelist. For three centuries the cathedral was the conventual church of the Joannites, known as the Knights of Malta, who between 1530 and 1798 assisted pilgrims travelling to the Holy Land.

La Valletta: In 1600 the Grand Master of the Joannites, Hieronymus Caraffa brought to Malta an excellent copy of the Madonna's image from the sanctuary of Picciano. When he was dying, he gave orders for the icon to be displayed at the Cathedral of Saint John. It soon became an object of great veneration.

La Valletta: The icon of Our Lady of Victories was brought to Rhodes from Damascus in 1475, and then in 1530 to Malta. Initially it was kept in the Church of Saint Catherine, but following the victory over the Ottoman Empire in 1565, Our Lady of Damascus was moved to a specially built sanctuary of the Victorious Mother of God. In 1931, on the four hundredth anniversary of the icon's arrival in Malta, the miraculous image was crowned with a Papal crown.

Mosta: The Basilica of the Assumption of the Blessed Virgin Mary at Mosta, glowing with lights, boasts one of the largest domes in the world. It has three thousand seats for believers, and room for ten thousand more standing. On the eve of the Feast of the Assumption of the Virgin Mary, it is surrounded by crowds of worshippers.

Mosta: The statue of the Virgin begins a procession – which will last for several hours – through Mosta. Thousands of cheering worshippers will follow its progress.

Mosta: The nineteenth century wooden statue was created by the sculptor Salvatore Dimech. It was completely restored in 1947.

SLOVENIA

This small country situated on the south side of the Julian Alps and on the Karst plateau, off the northern coast of the Adriatic, has rich Christian and Marian traditions, which go back as far as the second century. The Illyrian and Celtic tribes lived in the region which in the first century B.C. became a Roman province. The land was settled in the sixth century by a Southern Slavic tribe known as the Caranthians. It passed to the Franks, then the dukes of Bavaria, and in the end became part of the Habsburg Empire. After the Second World War Slovenia was made a constituent republic of Yugoslavia. It finally gained its independence in 1992.

The Slovenes are an unusual example of a nation and Church which existed at the crossroads of two great European civilizations, between the Greeks and the Romans. They were in constant danger of disappearing as a nation and losing their Catholic identity. Their beliefs were first threatened by the Byzantine, and later Serbian, Orthodoxy. Subsequently the country was dominated by Protestants in the days of the Reformation, and in the end by the followers of Islam. The Slovenes went through particularly harsh times during the German and Italian occupation of the country and the Second World War, and were subjected to brutal repressions by the Communist government. Around fifteen thousand soldiers who fought in the resistance against the Fascists were murdered, and many Slovenes were forced to emigrate. Dozens of priests were also killed, and hundreds were imprisoned. No lesser person than the Archbishop of Ljubljana, Anton Vovk, was covered with petrol and set on fire. Miraculosly, he survived the attack.

The Slovenes owe their devotion to the Virgin Mary to the disciples of Cyril and Methodius, the envoys of the patriarchs of the nearby Aquileia and archbishops of Salzburg. Western influence was always dominant in Slovenia, as testified by the oldest surviving texts in the distinct Slovenian language, which contain religious tracts.

Eighty six per cent of the Slovenian population is Catholic. During the Marian year, the Slovenes dedicated themselves to the Virgin Mary in a solemn act at the sanctuary of Ptujska Gora. Another important shrine exists in Brezje. During his visit there Pope John Paul II crowned the icon of the Mother of God, famous for the favours received through Our Lady's intercession, for the second time in the painting's history.

Zdzisław Szuba

Brezje: This Slovenian sanctuary at the foot of the Alps is famed for the image of Our Lady of Perpetual Succour.

Brezje: The photographs displayed at the sanctuary testify to the blessings received after prayers of Our Lady of Brezje. In 1863 four miraculous healings took place here, and since then the sanctuary has been attracting large numbers of pilgrims. The present church was erected in 1900, and in 1907 the miraculous icon of the Mother of God was crowned.

Brezje: The miraculous image of Our Lady of Brezje, the Patron Saint of Slovenia, is a copy of the painting by Lucas Cranach, produced by a Slovenian painter, Leopold Layer, at the beginning of the nineteenth century. During the Napoleonic wars he was imprisoned and sentenced to death. While awaiting execution, he made a vow that he would paint a Madonna for the church at Brezje. Five years later he was able to keep his promise when he was freed from prison.

SLOVENIA

Ptujska Gora: The national sanctuary of the Slovenes is sometimes also referred to as the Black Mountain, because according to legend it became invisible to the enemy during the Ottoman invasion. This miracle is supposed to have saved the lives of the local population, who took refuge in the Gothic monastery of the Franciscans, founded in 1239. The Communist authorities turned the monastery into a museum.

Ptujska Gora: The carving dates back to the early fifteenth century. It shows the Madonna, with an enormous cloak supported by seven angels. For centuries She has been sheltering with it all those who seek Her help in times of danger or need. She is the one who intercedes on our behalf and brings us solace.

In common with other Balkan countries, Croatia has gone through many changes of fortune. It would be difficult to understand the contemporary reality here, including the spiritual life expressed in the veneration of the Virgin Mary, without being aware of the area's history. Today Croatia is comprised of three historical regions: Croatia proper, otherwise known as Slavonia, Dalmatia and most of Istria. Dalmatia has the oldest Christian traditions. Christianity first arrived here as early as the second century. Pope Caius came from Dalmatia. He led the Church in the days of the Roman emperor Diocletian, born of a Dalmatian slave. Two hundred years later Christianity was already well established, as witnessed by the fact that the monumental mausoleum of Diocletian in Split was turned into a cathedral dedicated to the Virgin Mary.

In the seventh century the Ostrogoths and Awars were replaced on the coast of the Adriatic and in the area between the fork of the Drava and Sava rivers by the Slavic tribes of Croats. The disciples of Cyril and Methodius arrived there to spread Christianity among them. For a long time these lands were an object of both political and religious rivalry, between the Byzantine Empire and the Kingdom of the Franks on the one hand, and Rome and Constantinopole on the other. Finally, in 1075, after the coronation of the Croat ruler, Dimitar Zvonimir, by the Papal legate, the region became a fief of the Holy See and thus confirmed its affiliation to the West. Zvonimir's wife, Helena, who was a sister of the Magyar king, Saint Vladislav, founded a monastery and church at Solin near Split. Nowadays it is a well established sanctuary of the Virgin Mary, known as Our Lady of the Island. When the local royal dynasty died out, the kingdom of Dalmatia and Croatia was absorbed by Hungary. In 1527, Croatia, stripped of Dalmatia by Venice and of Slavonia by the Ottoman Empire, found itself under the Habsburg rule.

Catholic Croatia experienced yet another difficult period when it was part of the Kingdom of Yugoslavia between the wars, and after the Second World War of the Socialist Republic of Yugoslavia. In the days of Serbian tsars Eastern Orthodoxy became a dominant religion. Equally, the Communist authorities used all means at their disposal not only to supress the Croatian drive for independence, but also the activities of the Catholic Church. In 1992 Croatia finally became a sovereign state. Marian sanctuaries have always played a crucial role in the country's fight for freedom. Marija Bistrica, about thirty miles from Zagreb, is seen as Croatia's spiritual capital. In 1925, the thousandth annivesary of the Croatian Catholic Church was celebrated there.

Zdzisław Szuba

Marija Bistrica: The object of veneration in this sanctuary is the Mother of God, Queen of Croatia, crowned with Papal crowns in 1935. In 1715 the Croatian parliament decreed that a monumental votive altar should be erected here, in gratitude to the Virgin. It also decided to build a road for pilgrims from Zagreb, Hungary and Slovenia. In 1731 Bishop Juraj Branjung consecrated a new church, dedicated to Our Lady of the Snows. A statue of the Madonna was placed inside. The church was destroyed by fire in 1880. The present day sanctuary was constructed between 1880 and 1883, in the Neo-Renaissance style, following the design of a Vienese architect, Schmidt.

Marija Bistrica: The late Gothic statue of the Mother of God was moved here in the sixteenth century from the nearby chapel at Vinski Vhru. During the Ottoman invasion in 1545 a local priest had the statue walled up within the church wall, in order to save it from desecration. Forty years later, it was removed from its hiding place, but in 1650 it had to be walled up again. After its discovery in 1684 by a priest named Pietro Brezanica it was finally brought back to the church for good.

Marija Bistrica: The Cvjetko family has been coming here on pilgrimage for over forty years, and following the Way of the Cross round the sanctuary. Under the Communists, when organised pilgrimages were banned, whole Croat families used to visit their Mother, and pray for freedom for the country and the Catholic Church. Nowadays, around half a million pilgrims travel to the sanctuary at Marija Bistrica every year.

SVJETSKI DAN NE-PUŠENJA POD MOTTOM SPORT I UMJETNOST BEZ PUŠENJA 31.V 1996.	MARIJO BUDI UZ NAS OBITELJ VUČEMILOVIĆ	MAJČICE DRAGA ČUVAJ NAS MILAN HELENA NILER TANJA	MAJKO HVALA POMOZI I DALJE KRHAČ I.M.	HVALA TI MAJČICE ČUVAJ NAS I DALJE OBITELJ BROZINA 1995. OPATIJA	HVALA TI MAJKO ŠTO ČUVAŠ MOJU OBITELJ P. JURIĆ AUSTRALIJA	PEDESET GODINA 1942-1992 U BLIZINI OVOG SVETIŠTA HVALA ZA SVE M.B.B. DR S.D.	HVALA TI M.B.B. NA SVEHU ŠTO NAM DALA OBIT. E.I.I BRAĆE
BESCHÜTZE UNSERE TOCHTER I+H.W.	MAJKO BOŽJA HVALA TI ZA OZDRAVLJENJE MOJE MAME 1996. M.K.	HVALA TI MAJKO ŠTO SI ME VRATILA U ŽIVOT ČUVAJ ME I DALJE JOSIP	M.B.B. VRATI MI MARIJANA I DAJ MI SNAGE 95. MIRA	HVALA TI MAJKO ZAGREB 1995. OBITELJ RADELIĆ N.	MAJKO HVALA TI ZA SVE BUDI UZ MENE N.T.N	ZAGOVOROM MBB OHRABRENA OZDRAVIH HVALA MAJKO MICIKA M.CERČIĆ IZ KOMORA	M.B.B ČUVAJ NAŠU DJECU ANTONIJA A BORISA ZDENKA I MAT MIROHIJ 1995 TUZLA
BOŽE OČE NEBESKI DRAGI ISUSE I BL. DI MARIJO POMOZITE I DALJE A. VA.	MARIJO RASPRSILA JE TAMU SMRTI OKO ZENKE MATIJE ZAHVALNA M.S.B 1995.	SVJETLOST TVOJA MARIJO ŠTO SI SPASILA MOGA SINA ČUVAJ GA I ŠTITI I DALJE MAMA	SPAS ALANA U OLUJI ČUVAJ GA I DALJE M. ROPAC X 1995.	HVALA TI MAJKO ČUVAJ NAS I DALJE OBIT. JAGARINAC	HVALA TI MAJČICE ČUVAJ NAS I DALJE TONIĆA I LJUBICA 1994	DRAGA MAJČICE ČUVAJ MOGA SINA ŽELJKA I MENE ZDENKA HUDOLETNJAK	HVALA M.B.B. NA POVRATKU SINA IZ RATA I.V.
HVALA TI MARIJO B. ŠTO SI MI POMOGLA KOD OPERACIJE JA TI I DALJE PREPORUČAM SEBE I SVOJU DJECU Ž.J	HVALA TI MAJKO BLANKA	SV. MARIJO M.B.B. HVALA ZA SVE ČUVAJ NAS I DALJE 31.03.96. ZAHVALNA ADA B.	MAJKO B.B. MOLI ZA NAS OBITELJ JURIĆ	MAJKO BOŽJA BISTRIČKA HVALA TI NA POMOĆI OBIT. MEŽNARIĆ 10.95.	HVALA TI MAJČICE ZA SVE OBIT. BANFIĆ I OBIT. BOŠNJAK KRIŽOVLJAN R.	MAJKO MAJČICE HVALA ZA TVOJE DAROVE OBITELJ KOZINA H.V. M.M.M.V.	M.B.B HVALA NA POMOĆI NAŠE DJECE OBIT.KAMENJAŠE
HVALA MAJKO ŠTO SI SPASILA NAŠEGA VLADU U NESREĆI ČUVAJ GA I DALJE OBITELJ POŽEŽANAC	DRAGA MAJČICE I BUDI MI I DALJE NA POMOĆI M.B.	MAJKO HVALA POMOZI I DALJE M.G.	MAJKO B.B. MOLI ZA NAS OBITELJ ČVORIĆ	DRAGA MAJKO HVALA TI ZA SVE OBITELJ GRGIĆ 95. RADOVIĆ	M.B.B HVALA TI NA USLIŠANOJ MOLBI POMOZI NAM I DALJE LACKOVIĆ M. 95.	HVALA TI MAJČICE BOŽJA 4.IV.1995. STEFICA I MLADEN	M.B.B HVALA T NA POMOĆI OBIT. SCHRÖPF
MAJČICE HVALA TI T. N.	MAJČICE HVALA TI ZA SVE MARIJAN	HVALA MAJKO NA POMOĆI POMOZI I DALJE M.M.	HVALA TI NEBESKA MAJČICE OBIT. MAGLIĆ	NA ČAST M.B.B. ZA ZDRAVLJE I SREĆU JOSIPA ŠOŠTARIĆ	HVALA M.B.B ŠTO NAM JE SAČUVALA SINA MARKA PREPORUČAMO GA I DALJE TATA I MAMA NOVSKA	M.B.B. ZA USLIŠANE MOLITVE ZAHVALJUJE IVAN	HVALA TI MAJK BOŽJA ZA SPAS DRASK TOMI
HVALA KATICA i KRUNO	ZAHVALA ZA SINA I MAJKU M.B.B. I.I.I.	HVALA TI MAJKO I.I.	HVALA TI MAJKO OBITELJ ŽAGAR	MAJKO HVALA TI ČUVAJ NAS I DALJE I A GABRIEL AUSTRIA 1995.	PREPORUČAM NBB I SV. ANTUNU ZDRAVLJE DRAGICE MATIŠEV ĐURĐEVAC	HVALA TI MAJKO ZA SVE V. S.M. JURIĆ	MOLIM TI MAJKO B.B. ZA OZDRAVLJEN IGNAC I LJUBIC 1995 MARTIJ

Marija Bistrica: Stone or ceramic votive plaques are one of the indispensable elements of sanctuaries in Croatia, Slovenia, Italy and Belgium. They are a vivid testimony to the history of worship in local churches and the role played by the Virgin Mary in the spiritual life of the population.

Trsat: According to tradition, the Holy House from Nazareth was kept here between 1292 and 1294, before it was moved to Loreto. The miraculous icon of the Mother of God, brought over by the Franciscans, was a gift to the inhabitants of Trsat from Pope Urban V. In 1715 it was crowned with Papal crowns. The image is particularly venerated by the navy and sailors who arrive at the Rijeca port.

Sinj: This sanctuary was built at a place on the Adriatic coast where Eastern and Western influences meet. The Franciscans look after the icon of the Mother of God Full of Grace, which they had brought here in the seventeenth century. The painting, which belongs to the Venetian school of the sixteenth century, is famous for numerous blessings it has bestowed upon the faithful.

Sinj: The christening takes place at the feet of the Mother of God Full of Grace. Throughout their difficult history, the Croats have kept faith with the Virgin Mary.

Sinj: According to legend, the town owes its deliverance from the Ottoman siege in 1712 to the icon of the Mother of God Full of Grace. The defence of the city was led by a Guardian of the Franciscans.

BOSNIA AND HERCEGOVINA

Two once separate countries, which have always been located at the very centre of the explosive Balkan region, were brought together by their common tragic history. As Pope John Paul II said in Sarajevo when he arrived there after 1,300 days of bitter fighting, for centuries the area has been the place where East and West met, and often collided with each other. Difficult experiences of the Catholic Church, whose roots here reach as far back as the times of the Apostles, are part of the troubled destiny of these lands and mirror the devastation, and the dramatic fate of the local people of various nationalities and religions. More than half of the 830,000 Catholics who used to live in Bosnia and Hercegovina had to leave their homes. Out of six hundred priests, only two hundred remained. Many sacred objects were destroyed. The tragedy affecting contemporary Bosnia and Hercegovina is no more than an additional chapter in their turbulent history.

These two mountain countries were part of the Dalmatian province in Roman times. Like the neighbouring regions of the Balkans, they went through a period of tribal migration and were finally settled in by the Slavs in the seventh century. Bosnia was the first of the two to appear on the map of Europe. Since the tenth century it has been trying to shake off the yoke of Byzantium, Serbia and Hungary. The Bosnian rulers, called Bans, gained independence in the fourteenth century. Elizabeth of Bosnia, daughter of Ban Stefan Kostromanic and a Kuiavian princess from the Polish dynasty of Piasts, after the death of her husband, Louis the Great, made an enormous impact on the politics of Hungary, as well as Poland and Lithuania.

The country started to lose its sovereignty in the process of division into small principalities. A ruler of one of them adopted the title of Hercog, thus leading to the creation of the country named Hercegovina between the Neretva and Drin rivers. The mendicant orders, particularly the Franciscans, began to be very active in Hercegovina in the Middle Ages. They had helped Catholicism to survive during the

Medjugorje: A cross on the Mount of Revelations (Podbrdo) and pilgrims who have come to venerate the Queen of Peace.

Ottoman occupation, which lasted for over four hundred years.

The demise of socialist Yugoslavia opened the way for the growth of national and religious antagonisms. The phenomenon of the Virgin Mary's appearances at Medjugorje must be viewed against this background of conflict and violence. Since 1981 Mother of God, Queen of Peace has been calling on people to return to God, repent, pray and reconcile their differences. Not long ago the little village of Medjugorje was unknown to the outside world. It is now visited by pilgrims from many far off places. Pope John Paul II brought to Sarajevo a light as a gift for the Medjugorje Church of the Sacred Heart of Jesus. Until then, it burnt brightly in Saint Peter's Basilica in the Vatican, as symbol of solidarity with the suffering caused to the people of Bosnia and Hercegovina by the civil war.

Zdzisław Szuba

Medjugorje: The image of the Virgin Mary, who on 24 June 1981 appeared for the first time to six young people from the village, to ask humanity to strive for peace. Since that day, the *Gospa* (the Blessed Mother in Croatian) came back on several occasions, to deliver Her proclamations. As in 1917 at Fatima, She asked the world to return to God, to pray and fast. The picture, based on the testimony of witnesses, was painted in 1997.

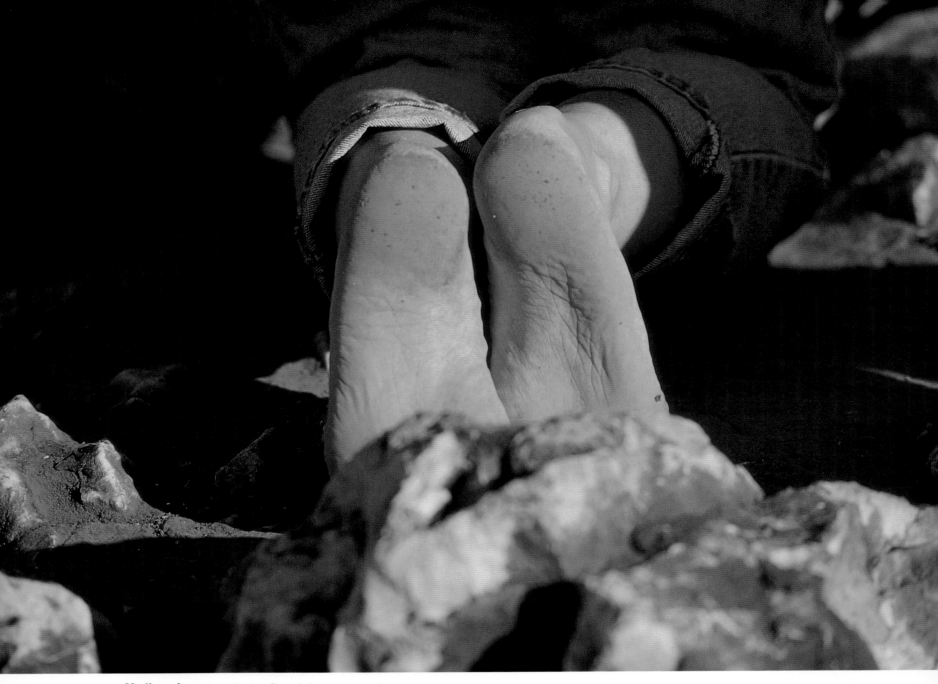

Medjugorje: Although the Church has not yet given a decision as to the worthiness of belief in the alleged apparitions, pilgrims from various parts of former Yugoslavia flock to the site where the *Gospa* appeared, to plead for peace in their countries, badly scarred by the war. It has become a tradition here to walk over the naked rocks barefooted or on one's knees.

Medjugorje: The news of the Virgin Mary's appearance spread rapidly round the world. Large numbers of pilgrims from all continents began to arrive at Medjugorje. Many people were converted to faith here. The number of pilgrims who visited the place since 1981 is estimated at twenty million.

Medjugorje: The pilgrims are rarely parted from their rosaries, a symbol of prayer to the Blessed Virgin. It was popularised in Europe by the Dominicans. According to a legend quoted by Blessed Alain de la Roche, the Mother of God instructed Saint Dominic to say fifteen 'decades' of the rosary, which are divided into three parts, each one containing five 'mysteries'. The 'mysteries' concern events from the lives of Christ and the Virgin Mary.

Medjugorje: Rosaries left by the pilgrims on the footpaths leading to The Mount of Revelations are wound round the feet of Christ on a Crucifix.

POLAND
LITHUANIA
LATVIA
THE CZECH REPUBLIC
SLOVAKIA
HUNGARY

POLAND LITHUANIA LATVIA THE CZECH REPUBLIC SLOVAKIA HUNGARY

At its dawn, Christianity emanated from the south of Europe towards the north of the continent. It arrived in Poland from Bohemia. From Poland it spread further to the north and east, to Lithuania and the Baltic countries. In this way, the substantial Slav territories were absorbed by Latin civilization. Although the nations who lived there experienced particularly violent historic upheavals, hostile expansion by their neighbours and numerous barbaric wars, they maintained their Christian roots throughout. Deep-seated faith, with attachment to tradition and the Mother-Church, expressed in everyday life and customs, helped to preserve national identity.

Jasna Góra (Bright Hill) (left):
According to legend, the icon of the Black Madonna was painted by Saint Luke the Evangelist. In 1382 Duke Władysław of Opole gave the painting to the Pauline monastery which he had helped to establish.

Mstów (preceding pages):
Every pilgrimage contains elements of penance and demands sacrifice, physical effort and self-discipline. The photograph was taken when a sudden whirlwind swept over the town of Mstów just as an open-air Mass for the pilgrims walking to Jasna Góra was about to begin.

Being situated in the heart of Europe has always been both a great opportunity and a curse for Poland. Opportunities arose from the fact that the country was traversed by ancient trade routes and its location made it open to new ideas, while the curse manifested itself in almost constant wars. Mongol hordes penetrated deep inside the borders and vast armies roamed from west to east and back again, leaving a trail of blood and destruction. As a result of its resistance to Mongol and Turkish attacks, Poland became known as the the 'last Bastion of Christendom', protector of the *antemurale christianitatis*.

The stigma of their painful history caused the Poles to seek protection and support in the Church. In particular, they expressed their faith through prayers to the Holy Mother of God, who was elected the Patron Saint of Poland centuries ago. Defenders of the Polish homeland marched with the name of the Virgin on their lips, under Her banners and with Her image on their gorgets. True to this tradition, in 1656 the exiled King Jan II Kazimierz Waza (Vasa) proclaimed the Virgin to be 'Queen of Poland' in Lvov. At the time, the rebellion of the Dnieper Cossacks led by Bohdan Khmelnytsky was seen by Moscow and Sweden as an opportunity to further their interests. Poland, as well as the Grand Duchy of Lithuania were both over-run by foreign armies. Three hundred years later, in 1966, Polish Primate Stefan Wyszyński renewed the pledge to the Virgin Mary at Jasna Góra (Bright Hill) in Częstochowa, during the celebrations of the thousandth anniversary of Poland's acceptance of Christianity.

The more famous images of the Virgin attract thousands of pilgrims, but there are also hundreds of less well-known pictures and statues of Her, scattered throughout the country. They can be found in lofty cathedrals and wooden country churches, in monasteries and road-side shrines, and invariably there are people before them, deep in prayer. Nobody managed to convey the infinite variety of these Madonnas better than Father Jan Twardowski, a talented poet, who in his *Polish Litany* wrote about the 'Melancholy Lady from Cracow's altars, granting favours to people', 'Young maiden from Lubawa, who conceals a resin tear under Her eyelashes', 'Swarthy mountain girl from Rusinowa Polana', 'Herb gatherer from Przydonica, found among ferns, juniper bushes and bilberries' or 'Fish catcher from the Swarzewo seashore, who will raise us in Her nets, high above our sins', and so many others, who reign in churches all over Poland, always ready to bring joy, consolation and relief from suffering, and to bestow numerous blessings upon the faithful.

Wojciech Niżyński

The sanctuary at Jasna Góra was visited by Pope John Paul II on five occasions during his pastoral visits to Poland. Before he was elected to the Holy See, he often came as a priest, then a bishop and a cardinal. He asked the Black Madonna to protect 'all those things that make up Poland, as well as the universal Church, and also all the continents and people who live in them'.

Jasna Góra: Polish Primate Cardinal Józef Glemp with Cardinals Henryk Gulbinowicz, Metropolitan of Wrocław and Franciszek Macharski, Metropolitan of Cracow, before the icon of the Mother of God, Queen of Poland. This miraculous image was crowned in 1717 with golden crowns given by Pope Clement XI. It was the first painting of the Madonna outside Rome which was singled out in this way. Most Polish kings have in their time come to pay homage to the Black Madonna.

Jasna Góra: After many days on the road, the joyous pilgrims enter the sanctuary of Jasna Góra in triumph. The last stage of the route leads through the Avenue of the Virgin Mary, laid out in 1818 as an artery connecting the old and new quarter of Częstochowa. Nowadays it is known as 'the great pilgrims way' or the most important *via sacra* in Poland. Over fifty different pilgrim routes converge on Częstochowa like spokes of a wheel. They vary in length from a score to nearly five hundred miles. Around fifteen per cent of pilgrims come from abroad.

Pilgrimage to the Virgin Mary: Fresh bread laid out by hospitable householders awaits the pilgrims along the way. The majority of them arrives on the most important Marian feast days: 3 May – Feast of the Mother of God, Queen of Poland; 15 August – Feast of the Assumption; 26 August – Feast of the Black Madonna of Częstochowa, and 8 September – the Birth of the Virgin Mary.

Pilgrimage to the Virgin Mary: According to tradition, pilgrims walking to Jasna Góra ask each other's forgiveness when they arrive at the apt-named Apology Hill. The priests are sometimes tossed up in the air, in gratitude for their spiritual guidance and care. Jasna Góra is just round the corner.

Jasna Góra: 'Mary, Queen of Poland, I am by your side, I remember, I am watchful...' – these words come from the Jasna Góra Appeal. On feast days dedicated to the Virgin Mary they are reaffirmed with the presence of a great multitude of pilgrims. On the 6th World Youth Day, 14 and 15 August 1991, two million participants gathered in Częstochowa at the invitation of Pope John Paul II. It was the first, historic meeting of young believers from West and East, who travelled here from nearly ninety countries.

Jasna Góra (overleaf):
The main celebrations of the Feast of the Assumption of the Virgin Mary, when absolution is granted to the participants, gather believers from all regions of the country. Annually, around five million pilgrims arrive here, many of them from abroad. People have been travelling to Częstochowa since the fifteenth century. The Pauline Order has been looking after the sanctuary ever since its creation. The priests who will be responsible for the sanctuary are ordained there.

Jasna Góra: Nuns from several different orders meet Pope John Paul II during his visit to Poland in 1979.

Jasna Góra: One of the traditions here is leaving one's medals and highest civilian or military decorations before the icon of the Black Madonna. Kings, leaders, as well as war veterans have been doing it for centuries. In 1977 soldiers who fought for Poland's independence offered to the Virgin a specially created image. The cloak covering the Virgin was made up from badges worn by various units of the Polish Army between 1908 and 1945.

Twardogóra: The Madonna who reigns in the nineteenth century church is known as the Mother of God, Help of the Faithful. The statue of the Virgin with the Infant Christ is especially venerated by those Poles who arrived in Lower Silesia from Vilnius and Lvov. The Primate of Poland, Cardinal Józef Glemp, assisted by the Metropolitan of Wrocław, Henryk Gulbinowicz, crowned the statue on 24 September 1995.

Kalwaria Zebrzydowska: The Feast of the Assumption, in the sanctuary of Our Lady of Calvary, also known as the Weeping Madonna. Kalwaria Zebrzydowska was the first Calvary (or Way of the Cross) created in Poland, and its layout is based on the topography of old Jerusalem. The complex includes the church dedicated to the Virgin Mary, a Bernardine monastery and Mount Calvary itself, with forty four chapels scattered over the hills. Inside the church, the mannerist retrochoir stalls with twenty six scenes from the Life of the Virgin, the richly carved mid-seventeenth century pulpit and the Baroque high altar all merit close attention.

Kalwaria Zebrzydowska: The architectural complex of the sanctuary is located among the picturesque hills of Lanckorona (representing the Mount of Olives) and Żaru (the Golgotha.) The construction of the ensemble was made possible by the generous donation of the Voivode (Palatine) of Kraków, Mikołaj Zebrzydowski, who between 1600 and 1621 funded the construction of twenty one chapels, the Chapel of the Crucifixion and the Chapel of the Tomb of Jesus among them. Members of the Bernardine Order have been looking after the sanctuary since the beginning of the seventeenth century. In deeply religious families, even very young children are taught to use the rosary during their prayers.

Kalwaria Zebrzydowska: Drops of blood, flowing from the eyes of Our Lady of Calvary, were noticed on the painting, given to the Bernardine Fathers in 1641. The veneration of the Weeping Madonna quickly became widespread. After the Partitions, the sanctuary at Kalwaria Zebrzydowska united the Polish nation whose country had been divided between three foreign powers. The icon was crowned with Papal crowns on 15 August 1887. Nearly a million pilgrims come to see Our Lady of Calvary every year.

Kalwaria Zebrzydowska: The crowds are particularly large during Passion Week and the festival of the Ascent of Calvary, during which the stories contained in the Bible are re-enacted. Pilgrims also arrive in vast numbers on the Feast of the Assumption, to follow the processions during which scenes of the Virgin Mary's funeral and coronation are staged. Before he became Pope John Paul II, Karol Wojtyła used to walk along the paths at Kalwaria Zebrzydowska in prayer and contemplation.

Kalwaria Zebrzydowska:
Reconciliation with God and the time we put our trust in the Virgin Mary invariably lead to spiritual rebirth. Kalwaria Zebrzydowska is a place where both Christ's Passion and the Most Sorrowful Mother *(Mater Dolorosa)* are venerated.

Kalwaria Zebrzydowska: Even mud does not deter the pilgrims...
The tradition of following the Way of the Cross was established
by Mikołaj Zebrzydowski. In 1632 the Bernardine Fathers initiated
the divine service, during which the participants walked along
the path of the Virgin Mary. It consists of three parts: the Sorrow,
the Dormition or Burial and the Assumption.

Kalwaria Zebrzydowska: Pilgrims
follow the path of the Virgin Mary
with a rosary in their hand. They pass
four chapels of the Burial and four
of the Coronation of the Mother
of God, which were funded by the
descendants of Mikołaj
Zebrzydowski. Saying the rosary
helps to comprehend the role that
the Virgin's presence plays in our life.

Limanowa (overleaf):
The 'sacred steps' lead to the
scene of the Crucifixion in the
so-called Coronation Square.
Stones from places venerated
by Christians in the Holy Land
have been embedded in the steps.
The penitents ascend the steps
on their knees, reflecting on
Christ's Passion.

Licheń: Priests are being ordained in the lower basilica of the sanctuary of the Sorrowful Queen of Poland. Since 1949 the Marianist Order has been looking after the sanctuary. It is one of the most popular pilgrimage destinations in Poland.

Limanowa (preceding pages):
The Gothic Pietà, showing the Most Sorrowful Mother *(Mater Dolorosa)* dates back to the end of the fourteenth century. Created by an unknown sculptor, it probably came from Hungary or Slovakia. In 1966 it was crowned by the Archbishop of Cracow, Karol Wojtyła. The crowns were stolen in 1980, and in 1983, now as Pope John Paul II, he crowned the statue again.

Licheń: In 1813 a Polish soldier, wounded during the battle of Leiptzig, had a vision of the Virgin Mary, cradling the White Eagle (Polish coat of arms). She asked that a painting of Her should be placed in the chapel. In 1844 an appropriate painting was put up in a shrine in the forest of Grąblin. Between 1850 and 1852 the Mother of God appeared several times to a shepherd named Mikołaj (Nicholas) in a place nearby. She urged the Poles to repent and reform. Since that time the painting has been held in great veneration. In 1967, Cardinal Stefan Wyszyński, known as 'the Primate of the Millennium', crowned the painting in a solemn ceremony.

Warsaw: For many centuries, Varsovians have maintained the tradition of processions progressing along the Royal Way during the *Corpus Christi* celebrations. One of the four outdoor altars, specially built for the day, is always erected outside the Church of the Assumption and Saint Joseph, originally part of the monastery of the Discalced Carmelites. It stands in Krakowskie Przedmieście, the first of the three roads which run from the Royal Castle to Łazienki, the summer residence of the last Polish king.

Warsaw: Behind its unusual facade, one of the earliest attempts to introduce Italian Neoclassicism to Warsaw, the Church of the Assumption and Saint Joseph houses an exact copy of a sixteenth century painting of The Virgin of a Happy Death. The original was a gift from King Jan II Kazimierz Waza (Vasa). It was destroyed in a fire during the Warsaw Uprising of 1944. The copy was painted in 1989.

Mrzygłód: At the close of the nineteenth International Mariological Congress which took place at Jasna Góra, the miraculous icon of the Mother of God Assumed into Heaven, Queen of Holy Rosary was crowned on 25 August 1996. The Archconfraternity of Holy Rosary was founded in the Mrzygłód parish as far back as 1644.

Mrzygłód: Pilgrims from the Family of Radio Maria, a station broadcasting religious programmes. Every year, they arrive at Jasna Góra, to renew their Pledge of Trust in the Blessed Virgin. They also travel annualy to Rome, to meet the Pope.

Limanowa: The Pauline René Laurencau wrote 'to say the rosary is to be united with the Virgin Mary in the contemplation of the Lord, who for our salvation was born of Her, died on the cross and rose from the dead'.

Kielce (preceding pages):
In pouring rain, the priests are waiting for Holy Communion at the airport near Kielce, before the coronation ceremony of the painting of the Mother of God, Full of Grace. The icon, dating back to the end of the sixteenth or beginning of the seventeenth century, was crowned on 3 June 1991 by Pope John Paul II.

Limanowa: Mother of God, like any true mother, knows how to listen, to understand and to forgive, She can give strength and revive hope. A moment of reflection before Our Lady of Limanowa.

Mrzygłód: Religious festivals dedicated to the Virgin are an occasion to show off beautiful folk costumes of the region, its culture and traditions.

LITHUANIA

Present day Lithuania is a relatively small country. History did not spare its inhabitants their share of dramatic events, humiliation and suffering. The arresting sight near Siauliai in Samogitia, known as the Hill of Crosses, is a symbol of this uneasy past. According to tradition, the local population began to erect votive crosses in the fifteenth century. The custom was revived when the Communists came to power. Thousands of crosses are a vivid testimony to the high cost of resistance to the process of sovietization. The Lithuanian Catholic Church played its part in this fight. Lithuania has been present on the political map of Europe since the thirteenth century. At the time it was a vast state, spreading from the Baltic to the Black Sea. It accepted Christianty only in 1386, as a result of its dynastic union with Poland. A peaceful conversion of a realm of this size had no precedent in those days.

For centuries Polish and Lithuanian nations had many cultural, social and economic links with each other. They were also united by their shared faith and saints. The Patron Saint of Lithuania is the royal Prince Kazimieras (Casimir), whose father was one of Poland's kings from the Jagiellonian dynasty. His remains are preserved in the Cathedral in Vilnius as holy relics. The Venerable Mykolas (Michael) Giedraitis, a monk from Cracow who died in 1485 and the Venerable Jurgis (George) Matulaitis, who was Bishop of Vilnius and who revived the Marianist Order, are also seen by the Lithuanians as their Patron Saints.

The Lithuanian dreams of independence came true in 1918, but they were cut short by the Ribberntrop-Molotov pact, when the country found itself in the Soviet sphere of influence. For nearly fifty years the Lithuanians carried on a bitter struggle, ignored by the world which had closed its eyes to the tragic fate of small nations subjected to totalitarian rule, and to their lonely fight for human rights and religious freedom. Marian sanctuaries helped to strengthen the sense of national identity. They include Siluva and the famous Gate of Dawn in Vilnius visited in 1993 by Pope John Paul II, who made an offering of a gold rosary to Mary the Mother of Mercy, as an expression of gratitude for delivering the Baltic States from the tragically misplaced utopia of Communism. Since 1990 Lithuania has been an independent state. Its traditional emblem – the Chase – has been formally restored.

Małgorzata Rutkowska

Vilnius: The Gate of Dawn. Since the seventeenth century the miraculous image of the Mother of God has been revered equally by Catholic and Orthodox believers. The Chapel of the Virgin Mary of Mercy is tiny, but the steps to it bear the traces of the feet and knees of thousands of pilgrims.

Vilnius: The chapel containing the painting of Our Lady of the Gate of Dawn is situated in one of the streets of the old city quarter. Passers-by often make a sign of the cross or sometimes kneel on the pavement. A replica of the Vilnius sanctuary was built in Poland, at Skarżysko Kamienna.

Vilnius: The miraculous icon of Our Lady of the Gate of Dawn, inspired by an engraving from the Netherlands, was painted between 1620 and 1630, and crowned in 1927. The votive garment is made of silver. It includes forty two rays around the Virgin's head and twelve stars.

LATVIA

Latvia is usually mentioned in the same breath with Lithuania and Estonia, as if the culture, history and customs of these three Baltic countries were homogeneous. This impression could not be more erroneous – in fact the differences between them were the source of their drive for independence. In the course of the twentieth century Lithuania, Latvia and Estonia appeared twice on the political map of Europe as independent, sovereign states.

In the twelfth century, the lands between the Baltic Sea and the river Dvina were inhabited by pagan tribes, such as the Cours, Semigallians, Livs, Sels and Letgallians. At that time, German settlers began to arrive there, first merchants, and after that Christian missionaries. In 1184 a German monk Meinhard came to Livonia, named after one of the tribes who lived in the area. Two years later he established the first bishopric in Riga. The Christian mission led by the bishops from Riga developed successfully. As early as 1205, Pope Innocent III referred to Livonia in his letter as 'the land of the Virgin Mary'. Her image appeared on coins, seals and princely coats of arms.

At the same time, Archbishop Hartwig founded an Order of the Knights of Christ in the conquered territories, popularly known as the Brothers of the Sword, on account of red crosses with swords on their white surcoats. They quickly joined forces with the Teutonic Knights. The Teutonic State survived in Livonia until 1561, when the last Grand Master, Gotard Kettler, converted to the Protestant faith and secularised the Order. As a secular prince of Courland, he saw the western part of the Teutonic State declared a fief of Poland and Lithuania, and the eastern provinces absorbed by the Polish-Lithuanian Commonwealth. This division was clearly reflected in the allegiance to two different Churches: Polish Livonia remained Catholic, whereas Courland and Semigalia were Protestant.

From the middle of the nineteenth century, Latvia experienced a marked increase in the awareness of national identity, finally declaring its independence in 1918. In the same year, the revival of the Catholic bishopric in Riga led to

Aglona: In 1840 the tsarist authorities turned a Dominican monastery into a prison for Catholic priests. During the First World War the building became a German military headquarters. In 1920 the whole complex was given back to the Church. When Latvia was annexed by the Soviet Union in 1940, the monastery was transformed into stables.

renewed veneration of the Virgin Mary. The old sanctuaries at Skaitskalne, Izvalta, Sarkani and Pasiena once more became centres of pilgrimage. In accordance with the Ribbentrop-Molotov pact of 1939 Latvia found itself within the Soviet sphere of influence. The Latvian people were subjected to repressions and policies of denationalization. However, compared with the Soviet republics, the relative freedom of religion was retained. The churches remained open, as did the seminary in Riga, which accepted candidates for priests from the entire Soviet Union. In May 1990 Latvia proclaimed its independence, which was recognised by most of the world the following year.

Małgorzata Rutkowska

Aglona: The Marian sanctuary at Aglona is known as the Latvian Częstochowa. It was founded by a bishop from Livonia, Nicholas Poplaski, who brought over Dominican Friars in 1699.
The monastery became a centre of Catholicism and Catholic culture in Latgale. According to legend, the icon of Our Lady of Aglona was painted by Saint Luke the Evangelist.
The Byzantine Emperor Manuel II was reputed to have given it as a gift to the Lithuanian Grand Duke Vytautas, who passed the icon onto the Dominican monastery in Trakai, in Lithuania. From there it eventually came to Aglona.

THE CZECH REPUBLIC

The Czechs, who over 1100 years ago received the mission of the 'Apostles of the Slavs', Cyril and Methodius, and through whom Christianity passed to neighbouring Poland together with the veneration of the Virgin Mary, are now one of the most secularised nations in Europe. Whether this state of affairs is a direct result of abandanoning the kind of spirituality associated with the Virgin and putting the emphasis on the veneration of local saints, is open to conjecture. In his testament, Cardinal František Tomášek warned against the tendency to move away from recognising the pivotal role of the Mother of God in Christian devotions. The same idea formed the basis of the aims that the Czech Church should strive for, devised by Pope John Paul II. During his visit to Hradec Králové, often referred to as 'The stronghold of the Virgin Mary', he said: 'Life with Christ is a wonderful adventure... Let Him, the Virgin Mary and your local saints become part of your everyday existence!' Many places which appear to have been particularly blessed by the Virgin have survived in the land of Saint Václav (Wenceslas). There are sanctuaries closely connected with the beginnings of Christianity in Bohemia, such as the supposed tomb of Saint Methodius in Velehrad and centres of worship from later periods, for instance Filipov near Litoměřice.

The spiritual capital of the country is probably Stara Boleslav. The greatest object of national devotion, the Václav (Wenceslas) Madonna, can be found here. The image is supposed to have been created at the express wish of Saint Ludmila, wife of the first Christian ruler of Bohemia. Her grandson, Saint Václav, wore it on his chest. Like many other paintings, it was destroyed by the Hussites. A copy of it was made and closely guarded against any further danger. Prague is the location of the most important of the fifty or so Loreto shrines founded in Bohemia in the seventeenth century. Its inhabitants set off on an annual pilgřimage to Príbřam, to Svatá Hora (Holy Mountain), the oldest and most famous Marian shrine in Bohemia. The Czechs also have sanctuaries which in a unique way bring people of different nationalities together.

Svatá Hora: Over three hundred steps lead to a Marian sanctuary which resembles a fortress. It stands on top of a hill, less than forty miles away from Prague. The shrine was built in 1673 in Baroque style. According to tradition, the Virgin Mary has been venerated there since the thirteenth century, when a knight called Malovec founded a small votive chapel, in gratitude for deliverance from highwaymen.

There are several notable pilgrimage centres devoted to the Virgin Mary in Moravia, such as Staré Brno, Křtiny, H. l. Masurky, Sloup, Vranov nad Dyji and Frydek-Mistek in Moravian Silesia. The heart of this historic region is dominated by the sanctuary of the Mother of God in Triumph, in Hostín. The Gothic statue of the Madonna with the Infant Christ is the object of veneration there. She holds thunder in Her hand, which She is supposed to have used against the Mongol invaders.

A characteristic sign of Czech and Moravian people's beliefs can be seen in the streets and squares of many towns or even villages. Baroque statues of the Holy Trinity and the Virgin Mary, sculpted in stone, were erected during the Counter-Reformation, as an expression of the old faith.

Zdzisław Szuba

Svatá Hora: The Gothic statue of the Virgin Mary with the Infant Christ had been kept hidden for a long time, because of attacks by the Hussites and of the Swedish threat in the years 1639 to 1648. Local legend says that the statue was made by the first Bishop of Prague, Arnošt of Pardubice. Nowadays the Madonna reigns from a magnificent altar, created from silver mined in nearby Príbřam.

Svatá Hora: The picturesque cloisters are richly decorated with stucco and painted scenes from the life of the Virgin Mary. The Jesuits arrived at Svatá Hora in the middle of the seventeenth century and built a wonderful Baroque monastery. A new church was consecrated in 1673.

Svatá Hora: The folk costumes worn during services at the sanctuary are proof of its close links with the region.
This tradition has been passed down over many generations.

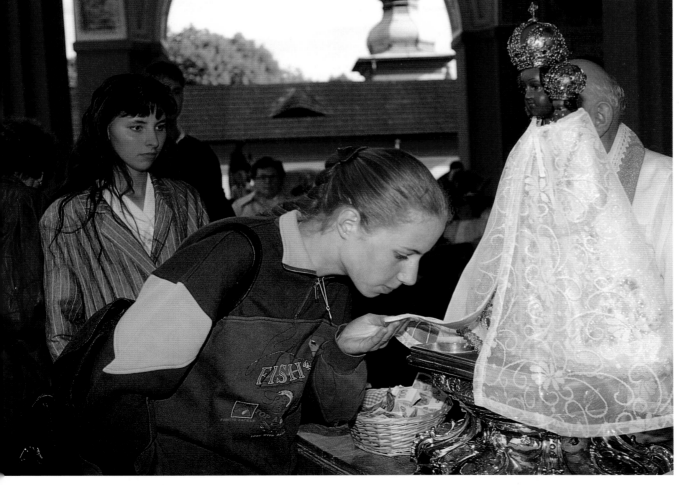

Svatá Hora: The first documented evidence of the veneration of the Madonna's statue at Svatá Hora dates back to the sixteenth century. After 1761, when the Jesuit Order in Bohemia was disbanded, the sanctuary passed into the hands of the Redemptorists. They in turn were removed by the Communist authorities.

Svatá Hora: Each day, after the main Mass, the faithful pay special homage to the Virgin Mary. While the Litany is being sung, they approach the miraculous statue of the Madonna, placed on a pillar before the altar, and kiss the hem of a gossamerthin cape which covers the sculpture. This has become a well-established tradition.

The Patron Saint of Slovakia is the Madonna of Seven Sorrows. Her famous sanctuary in Šaštín is located close to the current capital of the country, Bratislava. Slovakia became a fully independent state only in 1992. Despite continuous attempts by the Hungarians, Germans and Czechs to subjugate the Slovaks, they have managed to retain their national identity, largely thanks to their attachement to Christian faith, passed on to them by the Apostles of the Slavs, Cyril and Methodius. One of the characteristic features of their Catholicism has always been great veneration of the Virgin Mary. There are more than ten major sanctuaries dedicated to Her in Slovakia.

The shrine in Šaštín, famed for its sixteenth century statue of the Madonna of Seven Sorrows and the reverence that surrounds it, was described by Pope John Paul II during his visit as the place where the Virgin wants to act as a mother to all who come there, the place where everybody feels at home. After outlawing religious orders in Czechoslovakia, the Communists turned the monastery into an army barracks, and in every possible way tried to prevent the pilgrims from reaching their Patron Saint. Another Marian shrine which enjoys wide-spread fame is Levoča, the capital of Zips. According to tradition, it was founded at the time of the first Mongol attacks. Initially, the sanctuary was put in the care of Carthusian monks, brought there by King Václav, who ruled over the Czechs and Poles. During the Reformation the holy place fell into decline, but was gradually restored to its former glory by the Jesuits, who took over at the end of the seventeenth century. At the beginning of the nineteenth century, a Neo-Gothic church was built for the miraculous statue of the Madonna on the so-called Mariánska Hora (Hill of the Virgin Mary). When the Holy Father expressed in Levoča his wish that the Tatra mountains should bring people together rather than divide them, and tried to encourage his Polish compatriots to go on pilgrimages to Levoča, the inhabitans of Zakopane took note of the Pope's words. Every September they set off for Levoča from the sanctuary of Our

Levoča: At the foot of the High Tatras in Slovakia, on the borders of Zips, on top of the hill known as Mariánska Hora, rises a sanctuary dedicated to the Virgin Mary, the main pilgrimage centre in the country. Even when the Communist dictatorship was at its most oppressive, the Slovaks were not afraid to demonstrate publicly their faith and their attachment to Mother-Church.

Lady of Fatima, created in Zakopane's Krzeptówki. Slovak pilgrims follow the route in the opposite direction: from the town of Poprad to Rusinowa Polana, to venerate the Queen of the High Tatras. Yet another significant testimonial to the endurance of the Cyril and Methodius inheritance on the Slovak side of the Carpathians is the existence of the Greek Catholic diocese in Prešov, with its famous centre of piligrimage at Lunina. When the Communists tried to abolish it, even harsh treatment did not stop the local believers from remaining faithful to the Holy See. The persecuted members of the Greek Catholic Church found refuge in numerous, usually tiny sanctuaries, scattered throughout the mountains and containing icons of the Virgin Mary.

Zdzisław Szuba

Levoča: The Gothic statue of the Mother of God, gilded with gold, probably came from the workshop of Pavel of Levoča, a pupil of Veit Stoss. Since the late fifteenth century it has been housed in the chapel which according to tradition was built by the inhabitants of Levoča, to express their gratitude for deliverance from a Mongol attack. Many of the pilgrims who arrived here in large numbers experienced miraculous healings and other blessings.

Levoča: When the Communists were in power, the
sanctuary played a major part in maintaining Christian
faith among the Slovaks. Despite the official ban
on pilgrimages, people continuously made their way
to the shrine. In 1947 the Bishop of Zips, Jan Vojtašák,
in the presence of 150,000 pilgrims dedicated his diocese
to the Immaculate Heart of the Virgin. After Slovakia gained
its independence, on 2 July 1990, over 400,000 people came
to Levoča to thank the Mother of God for Her protection.

Levoča: When the whole family goes on pilgrimage, its members see it as an opportunity to dedicate their marital and parental love to the Virgin Mary. In this way, they express their gratitude, and ask for Her blessing and protection.

Levoča: The National Slovak Pilgrimage takes place on the Feast Day of the Visitation of the Virgin Mary. Frequently, the large clearing in the woods cannot contain all the pilgrims who arrive to venerate the Mother of God, wishing to be granted absolution. Many of them sleep on the ground among the trees, in order to attend Mass the next morning. For the past few years the inhabitants of Zakopane, in the Polish Tatra mountains, have been coming to Levoča to pray together with the Slovaks.

The pagan Magyars put an end to the Great Moravian Empire at the beginning of the tenth century. A hundred years later, they created the Kingdom of the Mother of God in its place. It was founded by the first Hungarian king, Saint Stephen, who was baptised by Saint Adalbert (Vojtěch) on the day the Assumption of the Virgin Mary is celebrated, and died on the same feast day. The crown given to him in 1000 by Pope Silvester II became the symbol of national unity. The former capital of Hungary, Esztergom, was the cradle of the Hungarian state and gave rise to the veneration of the Virgin. Saint Stephen and the kings who followed him were crowned at the Cathedral of the Assumption of the Virgin Mary there. For many centuries She was recognised as Queen of Hungary, with an official title *Magna Domina Hungarorum* (Great Lady of the Hungarians). Her most beautiful representation as a sovereign ruler, dressed in a Magyar folk costume, is probably the Rococo statue in the Church of the Holy Spirit in Sopron. Her emblems could be seen on Hungarian banners, royal seals and gold coins struck by the king's mints. For hundreds of years, the people of Hungary have been praying to their Patron Saint in the words of the traditional hymn: 'Our blessed Queen and Mother, our Lady over centuries past'.

Since the fifteenth century the country lived with the constant threat from the invading Turkish armies. Following a devastating defeat at Mohàcs in 1526, central Hungary, including Budapest, was turned into an Ottoman province for nearly two centuries. After the Soviet Army reached the Danube, the Catholic Church, which tried to resist the Communist terror, entered a particularly turbulent stage of its existence. In 1945 the Blessed Bishop Vilmos Apor was shot dead when he attempted to defend a group of women from soldiers who had attacked them. Many priests were arrested. The Primate of Hungary, József Mindszenty, became internationally known in 1948 when, having refused to let the Catholic schools be secularised, he was charged with treason and sentenced to life imprisonment. Archbishop József Grösz, who was threatened

Marianosztra: King Louis of Hungary, father of Saint Hedwig, founded a church and a monastery at Marianosztra in 1352. The royal family often came here from nearby Visehrad. The Pauline Order has been looking after the sanctuary since the fourteenth century.

with the possible deportation of thousands of monks to Siberia, signed an 'agreement' with the authorities in 1950. Religious activities had to be restricted to the confines of church buildings. Today, in the country where Saint Hedwig was born, there is a revival of interest in following the old pilgrim routes, including those leading to Pannohalma, where the Benedictine Order has been encouraging veneration of the Virgin Mary since the days of Saint Adalbert, or to Györ, famous for the miraculous icon of the Mother of God.

Zdzisław Szuba

Marianosztra: The painting showing the Mother of God – Our Lady of Hungary – is an eighteenth century copy of the miraculous icon of the Black Madonna from Częstochowa in Poland.

Mariapócs: The sanctuary in Mariapócs in the north-east of Hungary belongs to the Greek Catholic Church. The icon of the Virgin Mary which can be seen there is known as *Hodegetria* (The One Who Points the Way). According to tradition, on 4 November 1696 people attending Mass saw tears flowing from the Madonna's eyes. This phenomenon was repeated several times between that date and 8 December. The local parish priest was supposed to have gathered the 'precious pearls of mercy' onto a silk handkerchief and sent them over to the Church authorities in Egera, to be examined. They decided that the tears were real.

Mariapócs: The procession in honour of the Crying Madonna symbolises peace and reconciliation. At the end of the seventeenth century Emperor Leopold I had the icon transferred to Saint Stephen's Cathedral in Vienna, where it is still greatly venerated. A copy of the painting was installed at Mariapócs, where between 1 and 15 August 1715 it shed tears once more. It happened again for the third time in 1905, when the Virgin kept crying for over a month.

Mariapócs: Basilian Fathers minister to the pilgrims who arrive at Mariapócs from Hungary, Slovakia and the Ukraine. The Greek Catholic Order is based on the Rule of Saint Basil. The monks look after the Baroque church, built in 1731.

GREECE
BULGARIA
ROMANIA

GREECE
BULGARIA
ROMANIA

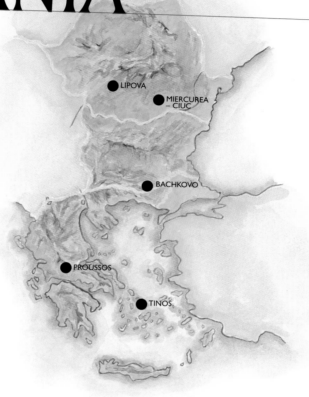

- LIPOVA
- MIERCUREA – CIUC
- BACHKOVO
- PROUSSOS
- TINOS

When one follows the coastline of the Black Sea and then proceeds towards the Mediterranean, one reaches the very heart of the Balkans, where for centuries Western and Byzantine influences and values met head on. To this day Catholic and Orthodox churches or monasteries standing side-by-side are a common sight. Stepping inside, they are almost indistinguishable, with their powerful aroma of incense and the candles flickering in the dark, refreshingly cool and mysterious interiors, filled with numerous icons. Every one of these churches has an image of the Virgin Mary – mother of all the Christians in the world.

Tinos   (left):
The icon of the Coronation of Our Lady of Kindness
(*Megalohari*), showing the Annunciation, was found by a nun
named Pelagia in 1822. It comes from the earliest period of
Christianity and can be seen in the sanctuary on the island.

The Bay of Corinth   (preceding pages):
The tiny chapel on an island, surrounded by water
and picturesque hills.

The numerous sanctuaries dedicated to the veneration of *Panaghia* (All Holy One), as the Madonna is called in Greece, embody the spirit which used to permeate all the Hellenic islands, and which still survives to some extent in places such as Nichori (Yeniköy in Turkish) on the Upper Bosphorus. The great poet of modern Greece, Constantine Cavafy, visited it as a child and later reminisced about it in one of his poems: *'If you would like to go with me to the Church of the Blessed Virgin Kumariotissa, I'll tell you what I think – I hope you will forgive my fanatism – but I believe that the entreaties of those who pray in faithful Nichori meet with a different kind of response than in other places'.* Despite the heart-felt preference expressed in these lines, *Panaghia* is revered equally in every Greek town, village or hamlet. The already quoted Cavafy described in another poem a sailor's mother standing before an icon in her house, invoking the Virgin: *'She places a burning wax candle at the Madonna's feet'* and even in sorrow feels at one with her Patroness, *'when the icon, solemn and sad, gazes at her from the wall...'* Icon or *eikon,* and *ikon* in modern Greek, means 'image' or 'likeness'. It can be found in every house which abides by long-established traditions. More often than not it is a representation of *Panaghia,* who reigns supreme particularly in Greek Orthodox churches. These paintings, even the simple peasant ones, are heirs to the glow of the ancient Greek idea of beauty. Unearthly yet familiar, it frequently amazes us, for instance in the human figures – and even more in the faces – of the so-called Attic *korae* in the museum at the Acropolis.

Travellers who visit Athens usually chance upon a small, enchanting Orthodox church in the street named after the god Hermes, near the crossing with the road known as Aeolus Way. This is the route which leads to the famous old cemetery of Kerameikos, where the greenery shelters statues blessed with perpetual youth and enormous colonies of tortoises, from miniatures the size of a matchbox to venerable patriarchs. The church bears the name Kapnikarea, whose meaning is a mystery even to present day Greeks. It may be derived from the word *kapnos,* which can be

Tinos: Tinos is one of the islands of the Cyclades archipelago in the Aegean Sea. As early as the first half of the nineteenth century it was recognised by a royal decree as 'the pilgrimage destination for all Orthodox believers', and in 1972 it was designated as a Holy Island.

translated either as 'smoke' or 'tobacco'. Perhaps there used to be a tobacco market in the neighbourhood. The cemetery has inherited its sobriquet from the ever-busy potters' (kerameis) wheels in this area. People who walk in its direction or simply shop in Hermes Street, generally stop by Kapnikarea, if only for a moment, and light a candle before an icon, to help the prayers on their way. I must confess that for me this church will now be associated for ever with the captivating way Greek women draw a sign of the cross on their foreheads and over their hearts. The golden dusk of Orthodox churches brings back images encountered in a dream, or maybe some long-lost childhood memories.

Zygmunt Kubiak

Tinos: During the most important religious celebrations, the miraculous icon of the Blessed Virgin is carried several times in a procession from the sanctuary to the port and back again. In 1831 the Church of Panaghia Evangelistria was built on the site where the icon was found. The image of the Virgin Mary was placed there, and soon became famous for the numerous blessings bestowed upon people and miraculous cures.

Tinos: Church dignitaries are awaiting the arrival
of the miraculous icon at the port. The image
of the Virgin Mary will be carried in a solemn procession
back to the sanctuary. The icon from the Church
of Panaghlia Evangelistria is also venerated by Roman
Catholics, bearing testimony to the shared faith
of the Western and Eastern Churches.

Tinos: The Virgin Mary's arrival at the port is greeted with dozens of ship sirens blaring. Our Lady of Tinos is the Patron Saint of sailors and fishermen, who hold Her in particular esteem. On Her feast day bishops bless ships and fishing boats, both docked in the port and out at sea.

Tinos: The youngest worshippers arrive in traditional Greek folk costumes. Thousands of people from all over Greece gather here every year for the great religious celebrations. On the Feast of the Assumption of the Virgin Mary, which falls on 15 August, the procession is joined by the high-ranking representatives of the government, the army, the air force and the navy.

Tinos: In a few moments the tired pilgrim will enter the shrine. The sanctuary is inalterably linked with Greek history, because the start of the fight for national independence coincided with the finding of the miraculous icon. In the chapel where it is housed, tiny ships and fishing boats made of gold are hanging on the wall. They express people's gratitude for answered prayers. An orange tree cast in silver stands near the entrance to the church. It was an offering from a man who miraculously regained his sight. He vowed to give the Virgin the first thing he was going to see after he was cured.

Tinos: The faithful follow the procession to the sanctuary on their knees, praying to the Mother of God for intercession. Later, most of the pilgrims will try to touch the frame of the miraculous icon, believing that at that moment a particular blessing will descend upon them.

Tinos: This pilgrim is making her way to the sanctuary from the port in Tinos. On her back she is carrying a child and a votive candle. The candle will be lit as an homage to the *Megalohari* (Miracle Maker) Mother of God. During the procession, the ill and the disabled who are laid out on the pavements along the way, pray for a miraculous cure.

Proussos: During summer, votive candles are lit outside the church. The pilgrims are given wine and sweets, which is also an invitation to make an offering of money.

Proussos: Pilgrims who are on their way to the monastery pause for a short prayer at the chapel built under the rock which bears the imprint of the Virgin Mary's foot. The chapel houses a copy of the miraculous icon, also known as the *Proussiotissa*, after the place where it originally came from.

Proussos: In the first half of the ninth century, the ancient Anatholian city of Proussa in Asia Minor was the place where an icon, believed to have been painted by the disciples of Saint Luke, was hidden in fear of desecration. A short while later, it was found in the mountains of Etolia. Very quickly, a monastery was built on the site. The earliest church was erected here between the end of the eleventh and the beginning of the twelfth century. The present one dates back to 1754. Until recently, the only way leading to it was a footpath. The road was constructed as late as 1969.

Proussos: According to oral tradition of long-standing, the Mother of God appeared here in a column of flame, leaving an imprint of Her foot in the rock. The miraculous icon was found in a nearby cave, hence its name — *Pyros,* which means a torch.

Proussos: Traditionally, visitors make an offering of money, always accompanied with a particular request to the Virgin Mary.

As early as the first century, Christianity arrived within the Balkan territory, which stretches between the Danube and the Rhodope Mountains. In Roman times the province used to be known as Thrace. The Church established a see in Sardica, which is today's capital Sofia. The Liturgy was celebrated in Thracian, and there were local Patron Saints, martyrs from the days of Emperor Diocletian. In the era of great tribal migration, Slavs who originated from the area on the banks of the Dnieper, had settled here for good. Towards the end of the seventh century they were defeated by the Bulgars from Turkey, who subsequently adopted their culture. Thus the Bulgarian state became the closest neighbour of Byzantium. For centuries the two powers were frequently at war, but the Bulgars only managed to retain their independence for short periods of time. In the twelfth century Pope Innocent III offered the royal crown to Tsar Kaloyan, and the title of Patriarch to the Archbishop of Trnovo. A significant role in Bulgaria's conversion to Christianity was played by the disciples of Cyril and Methodius, Saint Clement Slovensky from Ohkrida and his companions. Christianity in Bulgaria was seriously undermined by several centuries of Turkish occupation and by the Bogumils. The problem faced by the Christians was the support for the rule of the Sublime Porte among the Patriarchs in Constantinopole, who were subordinate to the Turkish Greeks known as the Phanariots.

In 1908 Bulgaria finally gained independence. Eastern Orthodoxy is the dominant religion. The Orthodox Church, is headed by the Patriarch in Sofia. It counts about eight million faithful in a population of nine million. The Roman Catholic community of less than 100,000 is only a small minority. During the inter-war years Catholicism in Bulgaria was mightily supported by the Papal Nuncio, Archbishop Angelo Roncalli, who subsequently became Pope John XXIII.

Orthodox believers in Bulgaria, as well as Greek and Roman Catholics, greatly venerate the Virgin Mary. According to a leading Orthodox theologian, Nikolas Zernov, this veneration is the very soul of

Bachkovo: The monastery was founded in 1083 by Grigori Pakuriani, who was Georgian and commanded the armies stationed in the eastern provinces of the Empire. To the Bulgars he was known as *Veliki Domestic*. A cemetery church, a handful of inscriptions and the monastic rule aimed at the Greeks, Armenians and Georgians, have survived from the period.

Orthodox devotions. Her image is always displayed in a prominent place of the iconostasis – the screen which separates the sanctuary from the nave in Orthodox churches. Every Orthodox bishop wears on his chest a medallion with the Mother of God (*Panaghia*). In June 1996 the Catholic bishops from Bulgaria went to Fatima, to dedicate their country to the Virgin's Immaculate Heart. A year later, a copy of Our Lady of Fatima travelled for six months between centres of Catholic worship throughout the land of the mission of 'the Good Pope', John XXIII. It followed in his footsteps of seventy years earlier, from Ruse on the Danube, through Plovdiv, Yambol, Chiprovtsi, Trnovo, Seymen, the famous Rose Valley (which is the source of one of Bulgaria's chief exports, the attar of roses, used in the production of perfume) and Varna, then on to Saint Joseph's Cathedral in the capital, Sofia, itself.

Zdzisław Szuba

Bachkovo: The miraculous icon of the Mother of God from Asenovgrad arrives at the Bachkovo monastery every year. The monastery remains open for the full twenty four hours, to allow the worshippers to pay homage to the Madonna.

Bachkovo: The interior of the
seventeenth century Orthodox
Church of Saint John, which houses
the miraculous icon of the Virgin Mary.

Bachkovo: The icon of the Virgin Mary was brought here
in a solemn procession from Asenovgrad, under ten miles away.
As in many other sanctuaries, the pilgrims try to touch the
miraculous image, often with a letter containing prayers
or expressions of gratitude for blessings received through
the Madonna's intercession.

Bachkovo: Exactly half way between Easter and Quinquagesima Sunday (last one before Ash Wednesday), the Orthodox Church celebrates the feast of 'division into halves', derived from Christ's teaching in the temple half way through Passover. During the festivities, the bishop blesses the water which is then taken home by the believers.

Bachkovo: The custom of bringing a lamb to church as an offering has survived in the Balkans, Georgia and Armenia. It probably dates back to the times when animals were sacrificed in the temple at Jerusalem. Occasionally the tree to which the lamb is tied will be used as *panikaidlo,* the stand for displaying votive candles.

Romania is the only non-Catholic country whose language belongs to the Romance group. Poised between West and East, it feels equally drawn to both. The language links it with the culture of the West, whereas the Orthodox religion ties it irrevocably with the traditions of the East. The inhabitants of Romania stress that unlike most other nations, they cannot really pinpoint the date when their country was baptised, as it has been Christian 'since time immemorial'. Indeed, the process of christianization began at the turn of the third century and carried on for hundreds of years. It was continued by the disciples of the Saints Cyril and Methodius. From the beginning of the thirteenth century, the veneration of the Virgin Mary became widespread in the principalities of the Danube Basin. Followers of the Orthodox Church and both Catholic rites – the Roman and the Greek – shared a common reverence for the Mother of God. Nowadays, over half the churches in Romania bear Her name. Icons of the Virgin can be found in almost every house and are the subject of great devotion. A light burns before them constantly, day and night. The Romanians, who have been tried so severely by history, pray fervently to the Blessed Virgin for their country's welfare.

The Romanian state, created through unifying several Danube principalities, appeared on the map of Europe in the nineteenth century. In 1878 the Congress of Berlin confirmed Romania's independence, even if the Balkan countries were denied some of the lands they wanted. The way lay open for further territorial demands and led, in consequence, to the First World War. In its aftermath, Romania gained Transylvania, which used to be part of Hungary, and also further territories in the north and east. The country had nearly doubled in size. The Carpathian Mountains separated the area once controlled by the Porte from the regions which had been almost completely spared the Turkish domination. The consequences of this division can be seen even now, for instance in local architecture.

For centuries, Transylvania was either ruled directly by Hungary or as a partial dependent. As a result,

Miercurea-Ciuc: This little town lies at the very heart of Romania, Transylvania, surrounded by the Carpathian Mountains. A Franciscan monastery was built on its periphery in the fifteenth century, and next to it, in gratitude for his victory over the Turks in 1442, a Transylvanian prince erected the Church of the Annunciation, between 1442 and 1448.

there is a sizeable Hungarian minority living in Romania today. Numerous German settlers also came to Romania, and were once very influential. The first wave arrived as early as the twelfth century. This ethnic patchwork is combined with the diversity of faith: Orthodox believers co-exist with Catholics and Protestants. The latter are mainly of Hungarian or German origin. Transylvania also has a Greek Catholic community. Its Church was created in 1698, following a union entered into in Alba Iulia, at the instigation of the emperor of Austria. The Communist authorities dissolved the Church in 1948 and it was forced to turn into a clandestine body. Since 1989 it has begun to reinstate its normal activities. 6.5 per cent of the Romanian population is Greek Catholic, 5.1 per cent Protestant, and 5.0 per cent Roman Catholic.

Rafał Górski

Miercurea-Ciuc: Between 1510 and 1515 the statue of the Mother of God was carved in limewood by an anonymous sculptor. In 1798 it was officially declared a site 'famous for its miracles.' An inscription was placed above it, which read 'Miraculous Mother, defender from the heretics'. It has survived a great fire in the church. According to legend, a Tartar commander who had failed to shift the statue, cut the Madonna's face with his sabre. These cuts are still visible.

Miercurea-Ciuc: Using the army, the ruler of Transylvania attempted to force his subjects to change their faith during the Reformation. Led on by their parish priest, the people met him in battle in 1567. They won a victory on the nearby hill, on the eve of Pentecost. To commemorate this event, a Solemn Mass is celebrated on the hill every year.

Miercurea-Ciuc: The Knights of Malta take part in the solemn procession from the church to the hill. Their Order, founded in 1113 in Jerusalem, still maintains its tradition of helping the destitute.

Miercurea-Ciuc: The family of Otto von Habsburg, pretender to Saint Stephen's crown, attends the celebratory Mass. Most of the congregation is made up of Hungarians who live in Romania. There are also Moldavians from eastern parts of the country, whose ancestors converted to Catholicism in the late Middle Ages.

Lipova: The small wooden Orthodox church stands on the site of an old sanctuary. It meets all the requirements of the Liturgy – its vestibule *(pranaos)* is lower than the nave, and it has an iconostasis. However, the screen is so tiny that it has only one door beside the central, so-called Tsar's doors, instead of the usual two.

Lipova: The miraculous icon of the Mother of God graces the Monastery of Saint Michael. It was placed in the centre of the iconostasis, which contravenes the normally observed strict rules, by having been constructed round the icon in a semi-circle. The image can be raised, leaving only the faces of the Madonna and Child visible through the round apperture, or lowered onto the Tsar's doors.

Lipova: The miraculous icon of the Mother of God at the Monastery of Saint Michael was probably painted in the seventeenth century. The Feast Day of the Assumption, known in the Orthodox Church as *Uspeniye* (the Dormition of the Virgin), is celebrated annually on 15 August and attracts thousands of believers from all over Romania.

252

Ukraine
Belarus
Russia

Ukraine
Belarus
Russia

TROKIELE
ŻHIROVICE
POTCHAIEV
KIEV
BERDITCHOW
MOSCOW
PERM

The Nestor Chronicle of the twelfth century tells how the Prince of Kiev, Vladimir, sent his envoys to the temples of several different religions. The Liturgy they witnessed at the Church of Hagia Sophia in Constantinopole proved to be a deeply moving experience: 'We could not be sure whether we were in heaven, or still on this earth.' And so in 988 Vladimir adopted Christianity from Byzantium. The Gospel and the Holy Icon reached the Kievan Rus'. The baptism became the shared heritage of the three countries who still see it as the source of their national identity: Russia, Ukraine and Belarus.

Kiev (left):

Orant – the thirty three foot high mosaic image of the Mother of God, at the eleventh century Orthodox Church of Divine Wisdom, is one of the masterpieces of Byzantine art. The inscription in Greek reads: 'God is in Her and will not abandon Her. May He support Her each and every day.'

Sergieiev Posad (preceding pages):

The monastery of the Holy Trinity and Saint Sergei Lavra was founded in the fourteenth century by Saint Sergei, who had a very high regard for the Virgin Mary. In 1744 it was elevated to the rank of *Lavra,* as a religious centre of special significance. Its spiritual influence spread over the whole of Russia.

From Kiev, where it was first adopted in the tenth century, the influence of the Eastern tradition of Christanity began to spread over the whole of Rus'. The Capital on the Dnieper became known as 'little Constantinopole'. The intention of the founders of Kiev's most magnificent church, Hagia Sophia, was that it would closely follow the ideal set by the basilica of the same name in Constantinopole. Countless churches were built as copies of Hagia Sophia throughout the immense territories of Rus'. In the twelfth century the miraculous *Eleusa* icon, later renamed the Virgin Mary of Vladimir, was brought over from Constantinopole to Kiev. In the eleventh century, the Mongol invasion destroyed the thriving religious centre in Kiev. After the country had finally shaken off the Tartar yoke, its devastated lands became the subject of intense rivalry between two powerful neighbours: Muscovy and Poland, and at the same time the terrain where Orthodox Christianity and Roman Catholicism co-existed. As a result of the Brest agreement of 1596, most of the Orthodox bishops active within the Polish State accepted the supremacy of the Pope, but retained Eastern religious rites and customs. The Greek Catholic Church played an important role in the development of Ukrainian national and religious identity. After the collapse of the Cossack rebellion, for several centuries the Ukrainian territory remained divided between Poland and Russia. The eastern part was quickly subjected to russification. In the west, despite sporadic efforts by Polish nobility to supress it, the native Ukrainian culture had a chance to survive and even to prosper. The tragic events of the Second World War revealed growing tensions between Poles and Ukrainians who lived in the region, resulting in armed conflicts and massacres. Under the Soviet occupation the Greek Catholic Church was made illegal. Despite persecution, it has managed to continue as a clandestine organisation. The emergence of independent Ukraine finally brought with it a chance of forgiveness and reconciliation. Today Ukraine resembles a virtual patchwork of religious beliefs and is not totally free from ideological and

Kiev: The Kiev-Pechersk *Lavra*. Dedicadet to the *Uspeniye* (The dormition of the Virgin) haused the earliest community of monks in Kievan Rus'. As far back as the beginning of the eleventh century, Christian hermits lived in the caves connected by subterranean corridos. The centre of pilgrimages existed here for several hundred years. In 1688 it was elevated to the rank of *Lavra*. The Communists turned it into a museum. In the independent Ukraine it once again became a monastery.

ethnic enmity. Central and eastern Ukraine is dominated by the followers of the Orthodox religion, united within the Russian and autocephalous or independent Ukrainian Churches. In the west, the Greek Catholic Church has come out into the open and was reborn. The Roman Catholic Church is also expanding throughout the whole country. Regardless of their nationality, Christians of all traditions are united in the deep-rooted veneration of the Virgin Mary, who for centuries has been worshipped equally by all of them.

Rev Michał Janocha

Kiev: The Kiev-Pechersk *Lavra*. The Icon of *Uspeniye* (The Dormition of the Virgin) shows the Virgin Mary finally at rest, and presents it as an example of the right way to die, which subsequently will lead to glorification of the believers. The Uspienski Church used to be the heart of the *Lavra* complex, but it was blown up by the Communists during the Second World War. However, the icon which portrays Christ carrying the transfigured body of His earthly Mother to heaven has survived. During *molebien* – prayers to the Mother of God – the icon is lowered.

Kiev: The Kiev-Pechersk *Lavra*. 'And God said, Let there be light: and there was light. And God saw the light, that it was good: and God divided the light from the darkness.' (1, 3:4) Since the very beginning of Christianity, fire and candlelight have symbolised life's victory over death and the glory of the saints. This explains the large numbers of candles, usually seen burning before icons in Orthodox churches.

Kiev: The Kiev-Pechersk *Lavra*. In the Orthodox Church, six psalms are read from the Psalter between evening prayers and Matins *(utreniya)*. During the reading, all lights except the candles are extinguished, as a reminder of the Last Judgement.

Kiev: The Kiev-Pechersk *Lavra*. As a symbol of the intimate nature of confession, in the Orthodox church the penitent's head is covered with a stole *(epitrachilion)*.

Kiev: The Kiev-Pechersk *Lavra*. The church dominates the banks of the Dnieper. It was built over caves in the hill given to the monastery by Prince Izaslav. According to tradition, the church was erected in the place pointed out by the Virgin Mary who appeared on a burning cloud before Saint Anthony and Saint Theodore.

Kiev: A bishop blesses the faithful with candlesticks: the one containing three candles symbolises the Holy Trinity, and the other, with two candles, the nature of Christ as both God and man.

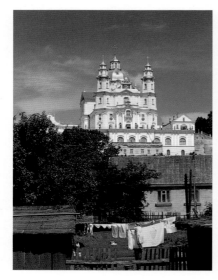

Potchaiev: The miraculous source of water and the icon of the Virgin led to the creation of a sanctuary. Its spiritual and cultural influence extended over the whole of the Ukraine. The magnificent church dates back to the eighteenth century. After the supression of the Polish November Uprising of 1830, the tsarist government replaced the Basilian Order at the sanctuary with Russian Orthodox monks.

Potchaiev: According to legend, in the twelfth century a shepherd saw the Virgin Mary standing on a rock and talking to a hermit. The Virgin left a footprint in the rock, and a source of healing water burst forth from it.

Potchaiev: The icon of the Mother of God is of Greek origin. It was given to the church in 1597 by Anna Hoyska. The image became famous for the many blessings that it had bestowed upon people. In 1773 it was crowned with gold crowns offered by Pope Clement XIV.

Potchaiev: The interior of the Orthodox Church of *Uspeniye*. In the upper part of the Baroque iconostasis there is an icon of the Virgin Mary. Many miracles have been attributed to Her intercession. It also commemorates the revelation which occurred in Volhynia.

Berditchov: Pilgrimage on the Feast Day of Our Lady of Berditchov. Her image is a faithful copy of the Virgin Mary of the Snows from Rome. Celebrations in Her honour have always united Ukrainian Catholics, those who belong to the Byzantine Church and the followers of Rome. In order to get here, some of them travel for hundreds of miles from the furthest reaches of the Ukraine.

Berditchov: This fortified monastery shelters the image of the Virgin Mary. The thick walls are a testimony to the past importance of the fortress. In 1630, Janusz Tyszkiewicz, a Polish aristocrat and a Voivode (Palatine) of Kiev, founded a church in Berditchov, in order to thank the Mother of God for answering his prayers and delivering him from Turkish captivity. He also gave the church a painting of the Madonna, which soon became famous for its miracles.

Berditchov: The founder of the church in Berditchov left the icon of the Virgin Mary in the care of the Discalced Carmelites, for whom he had a monastery built. In 1939, before the Red Army entered Berditchov, the icon was hidden away. Nowadays the services take place before a copy of the original painting.

BELARUS

In order to understand Belarus, one has to forget the idea of nationhood, formed over centuries of European history. Belarus never existed as a sovereign state. The people who lived in these territories ethnically and culturally belonged to Ruthenian tribes, and adopted Christianity from Byzantium. In the fourteenth century, the absorption of their lands by the Grand Duchy of Lithuania opened them up to Western influences and Catholicism. The union between Poland and Lithuania speeded up the process of polonization of Byelorussian gentry, while still allowing the local culture to develop. As in the Ukraine, the Greek Catholic Church played a major role in the growth of Byelorussian national and religious identity. The Partitions, completed by Russia, Prussia and Austria in three stages, in 1773, 1793 and 1795, resulted in the disappearance of the Polish-Lithuanian Commonwealth. In the area controlled by Russia, the Greek Catholic population of Belarus was forced to convert to the Orthodox religion and subjected to russification on a massive scale. The latter was made easier by obvious similarities in the two cultures. The russification and destruction of Byelorussian culture continued during the days of Communism. The wholesale murder of Byelorussian intelligentsia, carried out on Stalin's orders, still casts its tragic shadow over the nation's history. Whereas the Ukrainian Greek Catholic Church had managed to survive, in Belarus it stood no chance. The new independent Belarus is painfully searching for a way to rebuild its social and religious structures, cast as it is between Russia and Poland, East and West. After years of persecution, the followers of the reborn Christian faith, both Orthodox and Catholic, are looking for ways leading to reconciliation. The Virgin Mary, glorified in numerous icons and paintings, guides them along these paths. The veneration of the Mother of God has survived despite oppression, and those who believe in Her Son, although divided, often pray to Her together, as they used to generations ago.

Rev Michał Janocha

Zhirovice: According to legend, in 1470 the shepherds found a small carving of the Virgin Mary, made of jasper, in the branches of a pear tree. A bright light emanated from this image. On this site, a wooden chapel was erected, replaced in 1520 by a church, founded by the owner of Zhirovice, Jan Mieleszko. Members of the Basilian Order took care of the sanctuary of Our Lady of Zhirovice. The first Prior was Saint Jozafat Kuncewicz. The fame of the miraculous image of the Virgin attracted Polish kings, various potentates as well as ordinary people from Poland, Lithuania and Belarus. In 1730, the small (one and a half by two and a half inches), oval icon was crowned, amidst solemn celebrations.

Zhirovice: Over the centuries, the sanctuary shared the turbulent history of the surrounding area. In 1839, the monastery passed into the hands of the Orthodox Church, following the decision of the tsarist authorities. In 1918 Zhirovice returned to the newly resurrected Poland, and the church there was restored to the Catholics. Since 1945 it became again one of the holy shrines of the Orthodox faith. Nowadays the miraculous image of the Madonna is kept at the Church of the *Uspeniye* (the Dormition of the Virgin), and for the winter period moved to the Church of Saint Nicholas, built in the place where the icon was first discovered in 1470.

Trokiele: The first Church of the Visitation of the Virgin Mary in Trokiele near Lida was founded in 1500 by Marcin Gasztołd. The current church dates back to 1809. It has shared the harsh fate of the region and its inhabitants. In 1957 the Communist authorities closed the sanctuary, which was restored to the believers only in 1985.

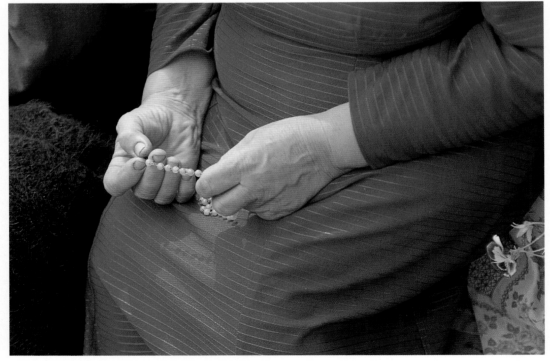

Trokiele: The rosary, held in work-worn hands. A few minutes given to prayer, spent reflecting the fate of the family and the history of the surrounding area.

Trokiele: The sixteenth century painting renowned for its miraculous powers, shows Saint Casimir, a Polish royal prince, kneeling before the Virgin. During the war with Sweden, the icon was miraculously spared. Under the Communist regime, people used to pray to it in secret. Nowadays many pilgrims again visit the sanctuary, particularly on the Feast Day of the Visitation of the Virgin Mary.

At the end of the tenth century, the light of Eternity fell on the hand of future Russia and penetrated the area. This Eternity was hidden in the depths of every human heart. Beauty had taken precedence over everything else – overwhelmed by the beauty of the Byzantine Liturgy the inhabitants of those territories had adopted Christianity. Slavonic gods were replaced by the Living God. The cult of Mother Earth gave way to the veneration of the one through whom 'the Creator becomes a child'. The descendants of those people were saints or sinners, conducting wars and erecting buildings, giving birth and killing, splitting into separate nations, within ever-changing borders. They were amazingly successful at creating a living hell for themselves and for others. But those who desired the Kingdom of God had no illusions that it could be attained through social reforms. They still thought of it as the incarnation of Beauty. 'Beauty will redeem the world', Feodor Dostoyevsky would write in the second half of the nineteenth century, and the whole Russian idea of aesthetics would testify to the truth of this statement. Beauty as the apogee of existence, free from temporal limitations and yet retaining details of earthly existence, became the standard everything else was measured against. In the Middle Ages beauty was not spoken of but simply expressed through the painting of icons.

An icon uniquely focuses the mystery, pointing the way through means of contemplation. Standing before it, a burning candle in their hand, the Orthodox belivers sang the words taken from the *Akathist*, the Byzantine hymn to the Virgin, as they do nov:' Hail, the ray of spiritual Sun'. In icons, Mary is almost never depicted alone, but shown as an advocate for all humanity, facing Christ on His throne. The icons where She is holding the Baby Jesus reveal an infinite love. God's tenderness, eternal and sherefore devoid of sentimentality is personified in the Virgin Mary. Although the heart is afire, it is watched over by the mind at peace: 'Hail, Love, rising above all desires'. Pilgrims prostrated themselves before those icons, unceasingly filling their souls with

Moscow: The Church of the *Uspeniye* in the central square of the Kremlin was built in the second half of the fifteenth century. Under the tsars it was the cathedral church of Moscow Metropolitans, and later of the Patriarchs of the Russian Orthodox Church.

Christ's prayer: 'Hail, Holiness, inaccessible to human mind'. Hermits would stand by them like living beacons: 'Hail the one who is permeated with faith in things so wonderful that they would be demeaned by mere words'. Seraphim of Sarovo, the great nineteenth century saint, would sing the *Akathist* every day: 'Hail the one through whom Joy shines'. Hail or *Ave* – which in literal translation means 'rejoice'. These were more than mere incantations. Every person in front of an image of the Virgin, would proclaim in the closing words of the *Akathist:* 'You are the one whose might is invincible'.

Irina Tartarowa-Hryckiewicz

Moscow: The icon of the Virgin Mary of Vladimir. This is the most famous of Russian images of the Mother of God. At the beginning of the twelfth century, it found its way to Kiev as a gift from the Patriarch of Constantinopole to the Kievan Grand Duke Yuri Dolgoruki. His son, Andrei, moved the icon to Vladimir. It was believed that on many occasions Russia had been saved from annihilation because of the prayers said before the icon. When in 1521 Moscow was spared from a Mongol attack, the icon remained in Muscovy, in the Church of the *Uspeniye* (The Dormition of the Virgin), within the Kremlin walls. Today it has been replaced by a medieval copy and the original is kept at the Tretiakov Gallery.

Moscow: The procession is encircling the Church
of the *Uspeniye* within the Kremlin walls. The celebration
of the *Uspeniye* is one of the feast days in the Orthodox
Church which are not movable. It falls on 15 August,
according to the Julian Calendar used by the Orthodox
Church, and ends the Orthodox liturgical year.
In the Gregorian Calendar this would be 28 August.
The occasion is marked by a solemn Liturgy, conducted by
the head of the Russian Orthodox Church, who blesses
the faithful with an icon.

Moscow: The Kremlin.
The magnificent interior
of the Church of the *Uspeniye*
was decorated by Russia's
greatest artists. The church was
built between the years
1475 and 1479. It witnessed
all the dramatic events in the
history of Russia. It is the
necropolis of Moscow's
Metropolitans and Patriarchs.

Moscow: The Kremlin. Many followers of the Orthodox Church believe that the Virgin Mary of Vladimir will lead Russia to victory yet again. This time She is going to help the country to overcome its inner chaos. For this reason, numerous people keep a copy of this icon, specially blessed by a priest, in their homes. They pray before it for peace in their homeland.

Moscow: The Kremlin. There are many forms of prayer. Some of them consist of constant repetition. The so-called *chotki,* or pieces of string with knots or beads, are used for this. They resemble the rosary of the Catholic Church, but the prayers are directed solely to Jesus Christ: 'O Jesus, the Son of God, have mercy upon us sinners.'

Moscow: The Kremlin. Alexei II, the Patriarch of the Russian Orthodox Church, leads a procession round the Church of the *Uspeniye.* The feast day of this name is one of the most important in the Orthodox Church.

Moscow: The Monastery of the Lord's Offertory. The anniversary of the date in 1395 when Tamerlane the Great abandoned the siege of Moscow is celebrated with a thanksgiving service, followed by a solemn procession round the church. Before the October Revolution, there was always a traditional procession from the Church of the *Uspeniye* in the Kremlin to the monastery, in which the icon of the Virgin Mary of Vladymir was carried.

Moscow (preceding page, left):
The Donski Monastery. The icon of Our Lady of Iviron is a seventeenth century copy of the icon found at the gate of the Iviron Monastery on Mount Athos. It is believed to protect Moscow from intruders.

Moscow (preceding page, right):
The 1593 Donski Monastery is dedicated to the veneration of the Virgin Mary of the Don. Her name is derived from the victory won by the amy of Grand Duke Dimitri Donski in the 1380 battle with the Golden Horde, which took place at Kulikovye Pole.

Moscow: The Monastery of the Lord's Offertory, which used to be closed under the Soviet government.

Moscow: The Monastery of the Lord's Offertory. Women are bowing in prayer before the icon of the Virgin Mary which is carried in procession round the church. For religious ceremonies, the icon is loaned to the church by the Tretiakov Gallery.

Moscow: The Monastery of the Lord's Offertory. A priest is blessing reproductions of the icon of the Virgin Mary of Vladimir, which have often replaced original paintings, destroyed by the Communists.

Moscow: At the end of the Orthodox liturgical year, the Patriarch of Moscow and All the Russias, Alexei II, blesses the worshippers with the icon of *Uspeniye* (the Dormition of the Virgin), on the annual feast day of that name.

Perm: A Russian Orthodox monk and a Catholic priest make a gesture of reconciliation during a mass in Perm, in the far eastern corner of Europe. Catholic and Orthodox believers live there in perfect harmony. With their hands, the priests shelter the flame, a symbol of life and continuity of faith. It is a sign of hope for Christian unity in the third millennium.

Conclusion

The Madonnas of Europe in their many guises reveal the same, unique *Theotokos* – mother of Jesus Christ, and through His grace, also our mother. Various spiritual and cultural currents and traditions gave Her face its features, dressed Her in distinct garments, placed different accessories in Her hand or at Her feet. The image which comes closest to the truth can be found in the Scriptures. The Virgin Mary appears in the first pages of the Book of Genesis (3:14). In the Proto-Gospel we come across the text 'I will put enmity between you and the woman, and between your seed and her seed; you shall bruise his head, and he shall bruise your heel.' The Books of the New Testament speak of Her on a few occasions, when She is waiting in hope and joy, when She is filled with trust and love or racked with sorrow and pain. In the last Book – the Apocalypse (12:1) we see the Virgin at the end of time: 'And the great portent appeared in heaven, a woman clothed with the sun, with the moon under her feet, and on her head a crown of twelve stars.' This biblical vision served as an inspiration to a Spanish diplomat, Salvadore de Madariaga y Rojo and the French artist, Arsen Heitz, when they designed the flag of Europe. The blue of the Madonna's cloak and the configuration of the twelve stars in Her crown were the motives which they consciously echoed in the symbol of our continent.

Whether the European flag is regarded from the point of view of heraldry, symbolism or geometry, its religious connotations recall our spiritual identity and Christian roots. Mary, the Madonna of Europe, present in countless sanctuaries, offers to succeeding generations the most precious gift She possesses: Her Son. She brings hope. She encourages gentleness. Her life and Her concern hold one message for contemporary Europe and the world: the last word belongs to love.

Rev Wiesław Al. Niewęgłowski

This book was published with the assistance of the Ministry of Culture and Art of the Republic of Poland.

SPECIAL ACKNOWLEDGEMENTS

H.E. Cardinal Henryk Gulbinowicz
Archbishop Stanisław Nowak
Bishop Jan Chrapek
Bishop Tadeusz Pieronek
Rev Metropolitan Bazyli Doroszkiewicz
Rev Prof. Michał Czajkowski
Rev Prof. Stanisław Olejnik
Rev Dr Kazimierz Kurek SDB
Rev Fr Marek Otolski MIC
Rev Fr Roman Tkacz SAC
Elżbieta and Stanisław Białaszek

Feliks S. Bruks
Leo Chu Chun Wan
Teresa and Jacek Czerkawski
Lidia Grabowska
Hanna Gronkiewicz-Waltz
Alicja Grześkowiak
Tom King
Lesław A. Paga
Ewa Pruchniewicz
Teresa Anton Rosendo
Stanisław Serdakowski
Dariusz Szołajski
Bogdan Tyszkiewicz

TRANSLATOR'S ACKNOWLEDGEMENTS

I would like to thank Rev Father William M. McLoughlin OSM, for his invaluable help, encouragement and unfailing charm throughout the lengthy process of translating and editing this book. All my thanks go also to Serge Bertini, who provided much information on European sanctuaries and geographical names, and was always patient and cheerful.

PUBLISHERS' ACKNOWLEDGEMENTS

The Publishers would like to thank the following institutions, without whose help this book would not have appeared: The National Conferences of Bishops of Austria, the Czech Republic, Great Britain, Germany, Ireland, Italy, Poland, Slovenia and Spain; Embassies of the Republic of Poland in Bucharest, Kiev, Moscow, Sofia and Vilnius; Embassies of the Republic of Bulgaria, the Czech Republic, the Hellenic Republic of Greece, the Republic of Latvia, the Republic of Lithuania, Portugal and the Slovak Republic in London; the Embassy of the Hellenic Republic of Greece in Warsaw; Kodak Poland; the Pallotine Travel Bureau; British Airways; National Tourist Organisation of Malta; FCB Jopek; Town Councils of Starogard Gdański and Tarnobrzeg.

We would also like the following persons to accept our gratitude for their help in preparation of this book:

AUSTRIA
Rev Fr Karl Schauer OSB

BELARUS
Rev Wacław Sudkowski

BELGIUM
Rev Lech Lewandowski

BULGARIA
Ewa Mładenow
Józef Kamiński
Romuald Kunt
Metodi D. Stratiev
Albin Szyszka

THE CZECH REPUBLIC
Rev. Dr. Tadeusz Fitych
Alena Juchełko

FRANCE
Stefan du Chateau
Zygmunt Sepaniak
Sister Katarzyna Skupień
Maja Zamoyska

GERMANY
Alois Furtner
Rainer Killich
Wilhelm Schatzler

GREAT BRITAIN
Archbishop P. Keith O'Brien
Sue Vincent
Rev Fr William M. McLoughlin OSM
Rev Fr Allan Williams SM
Rev Fr Brian Logue PP
Elisabeth Casper-Lee
Roger Lee

GREECE
Constantinos and Athina Karakotsis
Dimostenis Kaltsas
Sofia Riri
Anna Helder

HOLLAND
Patricia Ahlström-Klaver
Karel Klaver
Cyprian Kościelniak
Joanna Wnuk

IRELAND
Mons. Dominic Grealy

ITALY
Mons. David Lewis
Rev Fr Tomasz Ciołek ZP
Rev Fr Damian Delekta
Giovanni B. Figli
Rev Fr Konrad Hejmo OP
Sister Dominika Jędrzejczyk
Rev Feliks Kopydłowski
Rev Fr Paolo Melada OFM
Rev Fr Franco Ravinale

LATVIA
The Seminary in Riga
Beatrice Trueblood

LITHUANIA
Rasa Balcikonyte
Leonarda Orłowska
Andrzej Pióro
Jolanta Środa

MALTA
Karmenu Vella
Krystyna Mikulanka
George J. Hyzler
Rev John Sammut
Angela Said
Joe Camilleri

POLAND
Rev Dr Adam Bałabuch
Sister Teresa Banaszak
Rev Fr Grzegorz Bartosik
The Bernardine Sisters, Cracow
Sister Andrzeja Biała
Władysława Boroń
Adam Bujak
Anna Chmura
Małgorzata Chojnacka
Zbigniew Chojnacki
Lucyna Czarzasty
Agnieszka Dąbrowska
Małgorzata Dzieduszycka-Ziemilska
Maria Ernst
Marianna Falk
Janina Figat
Jerzy Foss
Krzysztof Gołębiowski
Cecylia Golas

Zofia Gondek
Elżbieta Górowa
Katarzyna Górska-Łazarz
Rev Józef Gorzelny
Rev Prof Marian Graczyk
Stanisław Grzonkowski
Zofia Gunia
Mirosław Heluszka
Mirosław Jarosz
Henryk Jusiewicz
Rev Jerzy Karbownik
Jan Kasprzycki-Rosikoń
Kasper Kasprzycki-Rosikoń
Krystyna Kierlanczyk
Jerzy Kołutkiewicz
Marian Konieczny
Magdalena and Arkadiusz
Kuśmierczyk
Stanisław Kuśmierczyk
Barbara Kurpiesz
Irena Kuszaj
Janina Lamot
Małgorzata Lech
Stanisław Leszczyński
Agnieszka Makarewicz
Cezary Malej
Tadeusz Matan
Rev Czesław Mazur
Małgorzata Mejer
Henryk Mikorski
Lidia and Andrzej Moszkiewicz
Michał Moszoro
Magdalena Nelke
Wojciech Niedzielski
Rev Prof. Piotr Nitecki
The Norbertine Sisters, Cracow
Jerzy Noszczyński
Barbara Nowińska
Emilia Osewska
Maciej Ostoja Mitkiewicz
Juliusz Ostrowski
Tadeusz Owczarz
Maria Pukowska
Renata Racibor
Stanisław Rosa
Prof. Antoni Rosikoń
Krystyna Rosner
Władysława Rzegocka
Hanna and Ryszard Rzepecki
Jan Sawa
Magda Siemińska
Marcin Skotnicki
Rev Dr Ireneusz Skubiś
Maria Sojdak
Rev Krzysztof Sojka
Henryk Solarz
Maria Stachurska
Prof. Klemens Stankowski

Prof. Witold Stępniewski
Bogusław Stopa
Piotr Stróżecki
Krzysztof Suchar
Jolanta Sykurska-Stachowska
Rev Dr Andrzej Świętczak
Joanna Tomas
Rev Grzegorz Trawka
Anna Turowska
Rev Fr Marian Waligóra ZP
Katarzyna and Jacek Wasilewski
Halina Wenzel
Rev Sławomir Wietrzyński
Ludwika Wilkosz
Izabela Wojciechowska
Wacław Woszczyk
Tadeusz Wrona
Maria Wyroba
Rev Robert Zapotoczny
Robert Zawisza
Elżbieta and Bogdan Żochowski

ROMANIA
Rev Fr Albert Bartok OFM
Beata Podgórska
Albin Szyszka

RUSSIA
Bishop Bronnickij Tichon
Rev Fr Grzegorz Cioruch
Natalia Dyachuk
Rev Andrzej Grzybowski
E. M. Jakowlewa
Włodzimierz J. Sandecki
Jurij Trubaczow

SLOVENIA
The Franciscan Friars

SPAIN
Rev Ramon Reñé y Bach
Manuel Garrido
Carlos Marrodan
Roman Mateja
Rev Fr Jean Andreu Rocha OSB
Krystyna de Salas
Mercedes Soley

SWITZERLAND
Rev Fr Wolfgang Renz OSB

UKRAINE
Archimandrite Pavel
O. Nestor
Jerzy Bahr
Bogusław Woźniak

BIBLIOGRAPHY

Azzopardi A. E., *Malta and its Islands*,
Plurigraf, Malta, 1995.

Bentley James, *A Guide for the Civilized Traveller*,
Bavaria, Aurum Press, London, 1990.

Biagi Enzo, *La Geografia di Francia*,
Biblioteca Universale, Rizzoli, Milan, 1982.

Castel R., *La Salette*, Editions du Signe, 1995.

Cruz C. J., *Cudowne wizerunki Najświętszej Maryi Panny*,
Exter, Gdańsk, 1995.

Crystal David (Editor), *The Cambridge Biographical
Encyclopedia*, Cambridge University Press, 1995.

Davis Norman, *Europe, A History*, Oxford University
Press, 1996.

Dejonghe M., *Roma, santuario Mariano*,
Cappelli Editore, Bolognia, 1969.

Delaney John J., *The Dictionary of Saints*, Kaye & Ward
Ltd, 1980.

Dopierała K., *Księga papieży*,
Pallotinum, Poznań, 1996.

Farmer David Hugh, *The Oxford Dictionary of Saints*,
Oxford University Press, 1992.

Fitych T., *Kościół milczenia dzisiaj*,
Agencja Wydawnicza „Czas", Praga, 1995.

Galli A., *L'Italia Paese di Maria*,
Editrice Ancora, Milan, 1992.

Galli A., *Madre della Chiesa nei cinque continenti*,
Editzioni Segno, Udine, 1997.

Garrido M., *Torreciudad Sanctuary*,
Editorial Everest, León, 1992.

Góral K., *Maryjnym szlakiem*, Biblos, Tarnów, 1996.

Guide de Tourisme, Michelin, Pneu Michelin,
Paris, 1998.

Hooper John, *The Spaniards, A Portrait of the New Spain*,
Penguin Books Ltd, London, 1987.

Ivanov V., *Il grande libro delle icone Russe*,
San Paolo, Milan, 1987.

Kevelaer, miejsce refleksji. Przewodnik i informator,
Kevelaer, 1995.

Knopf Guide, Rome, Italy, Alfred A. Knopf, Inc., New York.
Edited and typecast by Book Creation Services,
London, 1994.

Laurentin R., *Współczesne objawienia NMP*,
Exter, Gdańsk, 1994.

Levallois Marie Pierre (Editor), *En Bulgarie*, Paris, 1991.

Likhatchev D. S., Vagner G. K., Vzdornov G. I.,
Skrynnikov R. G., *La Sainte Russie*, Imprimerie Nationale,
Paris, 1994.

Marcucci D., *Santuari Mariani d'Italia*,
Editzioni Paoline, 1982.

Marcucci D., *Santuari Mariani d'Europa*,
Editzioni Paoline, 1993.

Mello Vianna de, Ferdinando (Editor),
The International Geographic Encyclopedia and Atlas, The Macmillan
Press Limited, 1980.

Monelli N., *La S. Casa di Loreto* – La S. Casa di Nazarett,
Loreto, 1992.

Owsijczuk W., *Ukrainśke maliarstwo X-XVIII stolit*,
Instytut Narodoznawstwa nan Ukrainy, Lvov, 1996.

Paliouras A., *To monastiri tis Panaghias ston Pruso*,
E. Tzaferis, Athens 1997.

Pasek Z. (Editor), *Miejsca święte, Leksykon*,
Wydawnictwo Znak, Kraków, 1997.

Potkowski E., *Zakony rycerskie*, Warszawa, 1995.

Rędzioch W., *Fatima i okolice*,
Pallotinum II, Ząbki k. Warszawy, 1993.

Rędzioch W., *Lourdes, Sanktuarium Maryjne*,
Pallotinum II, Ząbki k. Warszawy, 1992.

Ryszka Cz., *Od Ostrej Bramy po Fatimę*, Bytom, 1996.

Santarelli G., *Loreto, Its History and Art*,
La Fotometalgrafica Emiliana, Bolognia, 1987.

Scerri L. J., *Mosta, The Heart of Malta*,
Midsea Publication, Malta, 1996.

Tindal-Robertson T., Łaszewski W., *Fatima, Kościół
i trzecie tysiąclecie*, Warszawa, 1995.

Wormell Sebastian (Editor), *Czechoslovakia*, Pallas
Athene, London 1993.

Wormell Sebastian (Editor), *Poland*, Pallas Athene,
London, 1994.

Wysockaja N. F., *Ikanapis Biełarusi XV-XVIII
stagoddziau*, Belarus, Minsk, 1992.

Zaleski W., *Święci na każdy dzień*,
Wydawnictwo Salezjańskie, Warsaw, 1989.

*Z dawna Polski Tyś Królową, koronowane wizerunki
Matki Bożej 1717-1996*, Wydawnictwo SS
Niepokalanek, Niepokalanów, 1996.

LIST OF SANCTUARIES